1990

NEW ESSAYS ON WINESBURG, OHIO

★ The American Novel ★

GENERAL EDITOR

Emory Elliott
University of California, Riverside

New Essays on
Winesburg, Ohio

Edited by
John W. Crowley

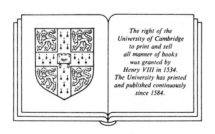

The right of the
University of Cambridge
to print and sell
all manner of books
was granted by
Henry VIII in 1534.
The University has printed
and published continuously
since 1584.

CAMBRIDGE UNIVERSITY PRESS

Cambridge

New York   Port Chester   Melbourne   Sydney

Published by the Press Syndicate of the University of Cambridge
The Pitt Building, Trumpington Street, Cambridge CB2 1RP
40 West 20th Street, New York, NY 10011, USA
10 Stamford Road, Oakleigh, Melbourne 3166, Australia

© Cambridge University Press 1990

First published 1990

Printed in the United States of America

Library of Congress Cataloging-in-Publication Data

New essays on Winesburg, Ohio / edited by John W. Crowley.
p. cm. – (The American novel)
ISBN 0–521–38283–1. – ISBN 0–521–38723–X (pbk.)
1. Anderson, Sherwood, 1876–1941. Winesburg, Ohio. I. Crowley,
John William, 1945–. II. Series.
PS3501.N4W576 1990
813'.52 – dc20 90–34340

British Library Cataloguing in Publication Data

New essays on Winesburg, Ohio. – (The American novel).
1. Fiction in English. American writers. Anderson,
Sherwood, 1876–1941
I. Crowley, John W. II. Series
813.52

ISBN 0–521–38283–1 hardback
ISBN 0–521–38723–X paperback

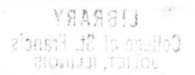

Contents

Contents

Series Editor's Preface

In literary criticism the last twenty-five years have been particularly fruitful. Since the rise of the New Criticism in the 1950s, which focused attention of critics and readers upon the text itself – apart from history, biography, and society – there has emerged a wide variety of critical methods which have brought to literary works a rich diversity of perspectives: social, historical, political, psychological, economic, ideological, and philosophical. While attention to the text itself, as taught by the New Critics, remains at the core of contemporary interpretation, the widely shared assumption that works of art generate many different kinds of interpretation has opened up possibilities for new readings and new meanings.

Before this critical revolution, many American novels had come to be taken for granted by earlier generations of readers as having an established set of recognized interpretations. There was a sense among many students that the canon was established and that the larger thematic and interpretative issues had been decided. The task of the new reader was to examine the ways in which elements such as structure, style, and imagery contributed to each novel's acknowledged purpose. But recent criticism has brought these old assumptions into question and has thereby generated a wide variety of original, and often quite surprising, interpretations of the classics, as well as of rediscovered novels such as Kate Chopin's *The Awakening*, which has only recently entered the canon of works that scholars and critics study and that teachers assign their students.

The aim of The American Novel Series is to provide students of American literature and culture with introductory critical guides to American novels now widely read and studied. Each volume is devoted to a single novel and begins with an introduction by the volume editor, a distinguished authority on the text. The introduction presents details of the novel's composition, publication history, and contemporary reception, as well as a survey of the major critical trends and readings from first publication to the present. This overview is followed by four or five original essays, specifically commissioned from senior scholars of established reputation and from outstanding younger critics. Each essay presents a distinct point of view, and together they constitute a forum of interpretative methods and of the best contemporary ideas on each text.

It is our hope that these volumes will convey the vitality of current critical work in American literature, generate new insights and excitement for students of the American novel, and inspire new respect for and new perspectives upon these major literary texts.

Emory Elliott
University of California, Riverside

1

Introduction

JOHN W. CROWLEY

*W*INESBURG, Ohio, it is sometimes said, appeals most directly to young readers. Its author, however was a literary late bloomer whose first book appeared only after he had turned forty. Sherwood Anderson, like the old writer in "The Book of the Grotesque," nurtured something inside him that was "altogether young."[1] As he wrote to the critic Van Wyck Brooks in 1919, "when in speaking of *Winesburg* you use the word 'adolescence,' you struck more nearly than you know on the whole note of me. I am immature, will live and die immature. A quite terrible confession that would be if I did not represent so much."[2]

The conditional phrasing of this "terrible confession" has been overlooked by those who would use it against Anderson,[3] for he was claiming in his "immaturity" to be nothing less than "representative" in the Emersonian sense, a Whitmanian seer and sayer of heartland America in its cultural adolescence. "My head is filled with fancies that cannot get expressed," he complained to a confidante at the time he was writing the Winesburg stories. "A thousand beautiful children are unborn to me. Sustained flights of thoughts break up and pass away into nothingness because I am full of the spirit of my times." His sharing "the very blood and spirit of all this aimlessness," however, was precisely what made him representative: "My struggle, my ignorance, my years of futile work to meaningless ends — all these are American traits. If I fail to get at anything approaching real beauty so have my times and the men of my times failed."[4] Anderson read his own writing, insofar as it did capture real beauty, as a representative triumph over the failures of his times.

Once, when asked by a Chicago newspaperman to summarize

1

his background, he reduced it to a narrative that was formulaic but potentially archetypal as well:

> About the biography matter. It is simple enough. Born at a place called Camden, Ohio, September 13, 1876 – I nearly wrote 1776 – spent most of my youth in the village of Clyde, Ohio, near Cleveland. Town poor family, village news-boy peddling papers, cheating people out of change etc. – all that stuff.
>
> Came to Chicago at eighteen – no work – common laborer until Spanish War broke out. Went into that.
>
> Stumbled into advertising writing and have been there ever since except for five years when I got the great American idea of getting rich. Started a factory – got all my friends to put money in – bright young businessman, etc.
>
> Scheme didn't work. Went nutty – had nervous breakdown – slight suspicion have been nutty ever since.
>
> Started writing for the sake of the salvation of my soul and except for one or two slips – when I fancied I might by some chance hit on a popular note – have been writing for that end ever since.[5]

This outline, in a staccato style that points ironically to the triteness of its details ("all that stuff," etc.), recalls the opening chapter of W. D. Howells's *The Rise of Silas Lapham* (1885), in which the slick reporter Bartley Hubbard, exemplar of a new school of vulgar journalism, is pumping Lapham for the details of his emergence from poverty and obscurity to a state of affluence and some degree of reputation in the world. This self-made man, the putative king of the paint industry, knows what is expected of him for this interview, which will lead to Hubbard's fulsomely flattering profile for the "Solid Men of Boston" series in a newspaper pitched to popular curiosity about the newly rich:

> "[S]o you want my life, death and Christian sufferings, do you, young man?"
>
> "That's what I'm after," said Bartley. "Your money or your life."
>
> "I guess you wouldn't want my life without the money," said Lapham.[6]

Certainly not, for as the reporter's satirical promptings show, he has already cast the life in terms of the traditional success story, extending from Ben Franklin through Abe Lincoln and Horatio Alger to the Great Gatsby and beyond, that is the most enduring in American culture:

"Worked in the fields summers and went to school winters: regulation thing?" Bartley cut in.

"Regulation thing," said Lapham, accepting this irreverent version of his history somewhat dryly.

"Parents poor, of course," suggested the journalist. "Any barefoot
business? Early deprivations of any kind that would encourage the
youthful reader to go and do likewise?"[7]

Hubbard and Lapham are agreed in their tailoring the biographical
facts to the rags-to-riches formula, which begins, in Hubbard's
retelling, with the hero's devoted parents (especially his self-
sacrificing mother), simple people of "sterling morality" who live
for their children's advancement and instill in them "the simple
virtues of the Old Testament and Poor Richard's Almanac."[8] But
the men differ in their attitudes toward this account. Whereas the
cynical reporter yawns over his notebook, the paint king warms to
the tale of his own success, revealing his reverence for what strikes
Hubbard as ridiculous.

For Sherwood Anderson, whose early life in Ohio bore uncanny
resemblances to Howells's experience two generations earlier,[9] the
rise of Silas Lapham foretold his own success just as Bartley Hubbard's mockery anticipated his own disillusionment with that success. The autobiographical letter quoted earlier may be understood
as a self-interview in which – as if he were playing the roles both
of Hubbard and of Lapham – Anderson parodies, even as he takes
seriously, the familiar story he has inherited from the nineteenth
century. But he is also transvaluing, and thereby recuperating, the
nineteenth-century idea of success.

In Howells's novel, Lapham's rise turns out, ironically, to be what
he gains morally from financial and social *failure.* Alarmed by the
corrosive effects of industrial capitalism on the human spirit,
Howells faced the possibility that morality and success were in-
compatible, indeed mutually exclusive. Anderson, who shared
Howells's abhorrence of industrialism, sought to write a narrative
of moral rejuvenation in which success could be rewedded to
morality. In his numerous and variant retellings of the rise of Sherwood Anderson, the literary artist supplanted the entrepreneur as
hero; or, in Howells's terms, the man of letters redeemed the man
of business.[10]

3

The "simple" facts of Anderson's biography, then, expressed a myth that was at once personal and cultural: not the nineteenth-century myth of success, but a modern reimagining of its terms. In his own eyes and in those of his admirers, his career became "the symbol of an epoch."[11] In a sense, Anderson became most truly himself when he was completely dissolved into symbol, when his life became indistinguishable from the myth of the artist-hero into which he wrote himself. As his biographer has remarked, "other writers draw on their experience, compose, so as to recreate, illuminate their lives, but always, apart from the perfection, or imperfection, of the work, there is the life. In the case of Sherwood Anderson one is never sure, one never knows which is which, or rather one knows that Anderson was never sure himself."[12]

Born in the centennial year of the American Revolution, Anderson was the child rather of the Industrial Revolution that transformed, during the very years of his youth, the agricultural, small-town Midwest. The second son in a family of five boys and one girl (another died in infancy), young Sherwood grew up in Clyde, Ohio, a town of about 2,500 that was to serve as the model for his fictional Winesburg. The family was among the poorest in town, largely because of the improvidence of Irwin Anderson, a sometime harness-maker and housepainter, a jack-of-no-trade, whose penchant for idleness and alcohol made him a thin provider. Enamored of military posturing and spinning tall tales – in Irwin's imagination, the Civil War, in which he had fought, was never ending – he, like Tom Willard in *Winesburg*, "swaggered and began to dramatize himself as one of the chief men of the town" (p. 44). In truth, he was a windbag who mortified his son and tormented his wife, the stoical Emma Anderson, for whom Sherwood, like George Willard for his mother, felt a largely unarticulated sympathy.

This sympathy, however, was copiously expressed – as if in compensation for childhood silence – in Anderson's later writings, where he sainted Emma by exaggerating her martyrdom to Irwin's vagaries. This mother-ideal, firmly established in Anderson's youth, governed his later relationships with women, including his four wives. He would never be entirely at ease with his own sexuality. Like some of Sigmund Freud's male patients during that same period, he tended to dissociate the "affectionate" current from the "sensual" current of erotic feeling and to divide womankind into madonnas and whores. "Where such men love they have no desire," Freud observed, "and where they desire they cannot love."[13]

In boyish rivalry with his father, Sherwood tried to distance and distinguish himself from Irwin not only by his sensitivity to Emma's misery but also by his attempts to relieve it through his own hustle and enterprise. In his desire to serve as the family provider, his zeal for odd jobs was indefatigable, his prowess as a newsboy unsurpassed. The villagers dubbed him "Jobby." Like Silas Lapham, Anderson imbibed the Franklinesque saws that passed for folk wisdom in nineteenth-century America: "Get on. Make money. Get to the top. A penny saved is a penny earned. Money makes the mare go."[14] These were the values that Anderson the writer would spend his creative life disavowing, but only after Anderson the businessman had pursued them to the edge of his sanity.

Ambitious beyond the limits of the small town, Sherwood migrated to Chicago soon after his mother's early death in 1895. The city had been booming since the Civil War; its population grew exponentially as its boundaries expanded and its industrial economy burgeoned. Hub of the Midwest, gateway to the Far West, Chicago challenged eastern cultural supremacy by erecting the White City of the 1893 World's Columbian Exposition, a showcase of the artistic and commercial aspirations of the emergent American imperium. Headquarters of the new captains of industry – the millionaires of meat packing (Swift, Armour) and manufacturing (Pullman, McCormick) and retailing (Marshall Field) – Chicago beckoned to immigrants and provincials alike, who, like Theodore Dreiser's Sister Carrie, flocked to a city enchanted by their visions of fabulous wealth. For the dreamers of success the sky was the limit, as it was for the architects of the skyscrapers that soon towered above the new business district, the Loop.

Anderson at nineteen (not eighteen, as he recalled) was understandably bewildered by the sheer magnitude of Chicago, and his upward climb was blocked by his inexperience and haphazard schooling. While he roomed in a boardinghouse owned by former Clyde neighbors, and later in a tenement with his brothers and sister, Anderson subsisted as a warehouse laborer at two dollars per day. Escape from the grinding ten-hour shifts arrived in 1898 with the Spanish-American War. Anderson eagerly rejoined the Clyde unit of the Ohio National Guard in which he had enlisted before going to Chicago; later he basked in a homecoming hero's welcome, although his unit had served in Cuba only after hostilities had ceased. During 1899–1900, he enrolled in the Wittenberg Academy in Springfield, Ohio; on graduation, with the equivalent of a high school education, he was offered a position as advertising solicitor with the Crowell Publishing Company in Chicago. Within months he moved to the Frank B. White Advertising Agency, later to merge with the Long-Critchfield Agency. Intermittently for the next twenty years, Anderson would retain his affiliation with this firm, even after he had achieved a literary reputation. His first writing, aside from ad copy, appeared in such trade journals as *Agricultural Advertising*, for which he produced a regular column under the titles "Rot and Reason" and "Business Types."

At this stage of his career Anderson was an unabashed booster of the mission of American businessmen, those who "sleep and eat and live with the desire to get on in the world tingling through their whole beings."[15] When, in 1903, he married Cornelia Platt Lane, the refined and attractive daughter of a prosperous Cleveland merchant, young Anderson appeared to have the world before him. Having shown a flair for advertising, he left the Long-Critchfield agency in 1906 to become president of the United Factories Company of Cleveland, a combine of small manufacturers. Anderson's task, less glorious than his title, was to organize direct-mail ad campaigns.

This was merely a step toward becoming head of his own sales operation, the Anderson Manufacturing Company of Elyria, Ohio, which was capitalized by believers in his promise as a bright young businessman. Through the clever promotion of a patent product for leaky roofs – "Roof-Fix" was guaranteed to cure every ill known to shingles – Anderson raked in the profits and ascended the business and social ladders of Elyria, a town with get-up-and-go worthy of Zenith in Sinclair Lewis's *Babbitt* (1922). Sherwood and Cornelia nestled into a comfortable house in a trig neighborhood, joined the golf club, and started a family (two boys and a girl by 1911). Anderson became a notable member of the Elks chapter and also the Round Table Club, a sociable discussion group drawn from the young married set.

Outwardly content, Anderson was inwardly restive. He began, in fact, to lead a double life: The gregarious man-about-town was also a recluse in his own home. Anderson installed a spartan workroom in the upstairs back wing, where he retreated to write – not the public musings he had penned for *Agricultural Advertising*, but the private visions of an inchoate artist. Far into the night and sometimes during business hours, Anderson wrote page after page, possessed by the stories quickening in his mind. He worked both on short pieces and on several different novels, two of which would appear in revised form as *Windy McPherson's Son* (1916) and *Marching Men* (1917). Through such autobiographical characters as Sam McPherson and Beaut McGregor, Anderson confronted his past and his profound uncertainties about the success he had so assiduously courted, a success that was being imperiled by the neglect of his business, which was sliding toward ruin.

Anderson's inner crisis had deep roots. Some part of him had always felt compromised by the advertising razzle-dazzle and the sharp business practices. His occasional lapses from marital fidelity – one-night stands with fancy women – were also symptomatic of an urge to be other than a respectable family man. In earlier years he had made fleeting contact with artists and intellectuals through his brother Karl, a painter, and he had been attracted to the openness of their lives and minds. Always a voracious (and indiscriminate) reader, Anderson sometimes flaunted ideas he knew deviated from those of his Elyria friends, who were incomprehending, for instance, of his enthusiasm for the radical philosophy of Friedrich Nietzsche. Through his own writing, Anderson unleashed a self at odds with those conventional values to which he was still tightly bound. He began to write, as he said, for the salvation of his soul.

Wound tighter and tighter by self-doubt and discontent with his career, his marriage, everything, Anderson finally came unsprung in November 1912. He later published several versions of what had happened one day in his Elyria factory: an exit that became as legendary in its way as Nora's slamming the door on her stultifying bourgeois marriage in Henrik Ibsen's *A Doll's House* (1879). In *A Story Teller's Story* (1924), Anderson recalled that he had gone to the office as usual and had begun to dictate business letters to his secretary. Unaccountably, he stopped in mid-sentence:

> What I did was to step very close to the woman and, looking directly into her eyes, I laughed gayly. Others besides herself would, I knew, hear the words I was now speaking. I looked at my feet. "I have been wading in a long river, and my feet are wet," I said.
> Again I laughed as I walked lightly toward the door and out of a long and tangled phase of my life, out of the door of buying and selling, out of the door of affairs.[16]

In his *Memoirs* (1942), Anderson explained that this strange behavior had been a ruse by which he hoped to extricate himself from his accumulated responsibilities: "Again I resorted to slickness, to craftiness. . . . The thought occurred to me that if men thought me a little insane they would forgive me if I lit out."[17] In truth, as the surviving records prove, Anderson was not feigning insanity; he had suffered a nervous breakdown. In a fugue state,[18] he walked out of his factory and, perambulating the countryside for more than twenty miles, arrived in Cleveland four days later, looking bedraggled and professing not to know who or where he was. The amnesia partially lifted during hospital treatment, after which Anderson returned home temporarily. Early in 1913, he liquidated his business in Elyria and, leaving Cornelia and the children behind, returned to his old job at Long-Critchfield. Determined at last to be a writer, he made his way into the literary worlds of Chicago and, later, New York. Shedding the chrysalis of the businessman, Sherwood Anderson the artist took flight.

So the legend goes. But the clean break with his old life that Anderson recounted in his autobiographies had been far more ragged in reality. For one thing, he could not simply or easily walk out on his family. He did undertake a searching reassessment of his marriage, deciding (unfairly, it seems) that his wife had discouraged his writing and smothered him with her genteel inhibitions. But a divorce did not become final until 1916, and only then on Cornelia's initiative, after Sherwood had declared his intention to remarry. For another thing, his progress as a writer was halting at first. The artistic quantum leap to the Winesburg stories, his first mature work, came only after a period of imaginative struggle.

Anderson's development was undoubtedly fostered by his association with the Chicago Renaissance, as it came to be called. Edgar Lee Masters, whose *Spoon River Anthology* (1915) was one of the inspirations for *Winesburg, Ohio*, recalled the intellectual ferment in "the really glorious year of 1914":

> The ideas of Ibsen, of Shaw, of the Irish Theatre, of advancing science, of a re-arisen liberty were blossoming everywhere, and no where more than in Chicago, where vitality and youth, almost abandoned in its assertion of freedom and delight, streamed along Michigan Avenue carrying the new books under their arms, or congregated at Bohemian restaurants to talk poetry and the drama.[19]

Through his brother, Anderson met several members of the artists' colony that was forming just at the time he was returning to the city: Floyd Dell, editor, critic, fiction writer, and apostle to the new Bohemia; his wife, Margery Currey, a teacher and reporter; the journalist Ben Hecht; the playwright Susan Glaspell; Carl Sandburg, an aspiring poet; Arthur Davison Ficke, an eccentric lawyer-poet; Tennessee Mitchell, piano tuner and free spirit, who would become Anderson's second wife; Margaret Anderson, bookstore clerk and founding editor of the *Little Review* (1915), which became one of the major organs (along with Harriet Monroe's *Poetry*, founded in 1912) of Chicago's literary avant-garde.

Dell especially made an impression on Anderson. Although a considerably younger man, Dell regarded Anderson as a protégé and acted as his mentor. He took it upon himself to get *Windy McPherson's Son* into print by urging it on Dreiser's publisher, John Lane. Dell also introduced Anderson to psychoanalysis, at least in the vague and somewhat distorted form in which Freud's ideas were filtering into America. Another discovery at that time was Gertrude Stein, whose oracular *Tender Buttons* (1914) pointed Anderson toward the narrative complexity and vernacular grace of *Winesburg*.

Throughout 1914 and 1915, Anderson juggled his own work with his ad writing, living sparely in a midtown boardinghouse at 735 Cass Street. Like the old writer in "The Book of the Grotesque," he had his bed raised to window level so that he might observe the street life below and then ponder his relationship to the people espied from this perch or encountered as he roamed the city. The situation of the artist became the theme of the novel he was drafting about the growth of a writer like himself. *Talbot Whittingham*, which was never published, reveals much about Anderson's continuing self-division. His removal from Elyria had not reduced the friction in his daily life caused by his double career as a man of letters and a man of business, by his incongruous allegiances to a liberated artistic circle and to his conservative advertising contacts. Nor had Anderson clarified his conception of himself as a writer.

Walter B. Rideout has argued that *Talbot Whittingham* dramatizes a conflict between two artistic ideals: a severe Nietzschean "master artist" who speaks for a world from which he feels necessarily alienated versus a compassionate Whitmanian bard whose art germinates from his imaginative embrace of the democratic en masse.[20] Talbot eventually discovers, in Rideout's words, the principles that "grotesqueness . . . is a universal but outward condition of the world which both defeats men's dreams and separates them as individuals; beauty is a universal but inward condition which exists beyond defeat, binds individuals into a community, and when liberated by the artist's insight, emerges out of defeat in the form of art."[21]

Thus, the artist is empowered to speak for the grotesques only by taking his place among them. As Anderson asked himself rhetorically in a 1917 letter, "Am I to become one who takes himself seriously and talks of his work as though it were the manna of Heaven instead of just the scribbling of one poor twisted human in the midst of a world of twisted ones."[22] The latter artistic ethos, which David Stouck (later in this volume) calls Anderson's expressionism, prevailed in *Winesburg*. Here Dr. Reefy's wife learns the saving secret of "the sweetness of the twisted apples" (p. 38), a secret that was revealed to Anderson late in 1915.

Like his exit from Elyria, Anderson's writing of *Winesburg, Ohio* became a legend in his own time – and in his own mind. He never ceased recounting, in ever more fanciful detail, the miraculous moment of inspiration. In his final version, in the *Memoirs*, Anderson recalled a rainy night in late fall when he had gone to bed without pajamas:

I was there naked in the bed and I sprang up. I went to my typewriter and began to write. It was there, under those circumstances, myself sitting near an open window, the rain occasionally blowing in and wetting my bare back, that I did my first writing. I wrote the first of the stories, afterwards to be known as the Winesburg stories. I wrote it, as I wrote them all, complete in the one sitting. I do not think I afterwards changed a word of it. . . . The rest of the stories in the book came out of me on succeeding evenings, and sometimes during the day while I worked in the advertising office. At intervals there would be a blank space of a week, and then there would be two or three written during a week. I was like a woman having my babies, one after another but without pain.[23]

As William L. Phillips has shown, there is little in these paragraphs that is strictly accurate.[24] The stories were written in pencil, not typed; the first of them was not "Hands," as Anderson often stated, but "The Book of the Grotesque"; the manuscript contains many changed words. However fictional in its particulars, the tale does bear an essential truth: that *Winesburg* was written in a state of rapture, as if Anderson had been a virgin seminally visited by the gods within. His imagery suggests that the stories resulted not simply from parthenogenesis but, what is equally remarkable, from painless multiple parturition.

Anderson's imagining himself as a woman is central to his idea of the artist, for he was consciously in revolt against the model of manhood he had adopted in his youth. Part of what made *Winesburg, Ohio* seem so "modern" to its first readers was its questioning of Victorian gender codes, which in fact had been steadily losing the authority that once had enforced a clear separation between the domestic sphere of women and the encompassing world of men. During the same period in which Anderson pursued his business career, the old roles were under mounting criticism from both men and women: "Benevolent patriarchy at home imposed upon many wives a despotism by harshness or neglect or both. Heroic and honorable achievement outside the home, meanwhile, seemed to many men an increasingly elusive goal. Feminist agitation coincided with male doubts about the traditional manliness ideal, thereby creating not only a battle of the sexes, but also a psychic civil war among men."[25] As Anderson was later to recognize, his Elyria crisis had been representative. He had been only one of many American men who no longer found fulfillment in work that seemed unsatisfying and enervating, who no longer knew exactly what to think of themselves as men.

Anderson, however, did not gravitate to the "virile" masculine ideal that was epitomized in Theodore Roosevelt's preachments for "the strenuous life."[26] Rather, he explored what he regarded as his "womanly" capacity to be receptive to the experience of others. As Kim Townsend remarks, "what Anderson saw was that any man who did not question the manhood that he achieved, did not keep alive the possibility or the expectation of something better, would be less than a man. He would be only that churlish, dogged figure that had no sympathy for others, least of all anything 'other' in himself." As a writer, he espoused a form of narrative that, as in "Hands," was "not focused, not building to a climax, not phallic, as it were, but weaving gracefully back and forth between past and present, between its business and digressions."[27]

Although many of the stories in *Winesburg, Ohio* reflect Anderson's sensitivity to the plight of women in American society, and although he was supportive of women's seeking new gender arrangements, he was not a "feminist," as the term was understood either in his time or in ours. More precisely, he was an anti-anti-feminist, a man not so much *for* women as against those who obviously oppressed them, a man ultimately concerned with redefining his own masculinity in positive terms, which might mean acceptance, however chary, of homosexuality.

In one version of his writing of "Hands," for instance, Anderson recalled that he and another frustrated writer at the agency – men joined by their contempt for the advertising business that supported but also threatened their artistic integrity – used to call each other by women's names: "In recognition of our common harlotry he was 'Little Eva' as I was 'Mabel.'"[28] After a round of the bars one afternoon, during which "Mabel" and "Little Eva" were eyed as "a pair of fairies," Anderson returned drunk to his room and then experienced a vision, induced by the play of light from a street lamp on the bare wall. Distinct faces began to appear, the faces of ordinary people whose lives were tragic:

Among the figures on the wall there had been one of a little fright-ened man. Perhaps it came out of some memory of my own, a face seen sometimes on the street, a story told by some man in a bar-room, as well as out of the experience that very day, the fat man calling me 'Mabel,' me calling him 'Eva,' and our suspiciousness in the eyes of other men, hangers-on in the cheap barrooms. But something else was mixed in it. Out of them seemed to speak the passionate desire in all people to be understood, to have their stories told, perhaps that the terrible isolation of their lives may break. I went to my table and began writing. The story is called "Hands"; it is in *Winesburg*.[29]

Anderson identifies himself at first with another "fairy," an incip-ient Wing Biddlebaum, but his focus then shifts to a generalized awareness of the "terrible isolation" in the lives of "all people," including the suspicious hangers-on. As Thomas Yingling argues (later in this volume), the narrative logic of *Winesburg, Ohio*, like the logic of this passage, finally upholds a heterosexual hegemony by assimilating the "otherness" of one little frightened man into the "universal" condition of all men. There is no doubt that An-derson as "Mabel" the harlot was playing a role that − however sympathetic he may have felt toward women and homosexuals − was fundamentally sexist and homophobic. But having noted this, it is still possible to credit Anderson's desire in *Winesburg* to explore the boundary between "man" and "woman," to expand the hori-zon of his own masculinity to a point where all gender differences might blur into a pansexuality that is finally nongenital, for, like Wing Biddlebaum, Anderson was "one of those men in whom the force that creates life is diffused, not centralized" (p. 32).

To the writer Edward Dahlberg, Anderson was a "sex visionary" in the Whitmanian mode, one who confirmed the "profound ob-servation" in the gospel of John "that the truthseeker is without pity, but the sensual man sorrows for others." Because Anderson's "flesh was always growing and ripening for others," says Dahlberg, his "aching skin took the place of what we others call mind, but which is more important than the human brain, because it is infinitely more loving. One does not have to be afraid of a mead-ow, which can't hurt you; what is to be dreaded is the mind without feeling, for it is a most malignant faculty."[30]

The Winesburg stories were written mindlessly, as it were, by Anderson's "aching skin." He once expressed the wish that "nothing from my pen should be published that could not be read aloud in the presence of a cornfield."[31] Ideally, the writer should be as organic as the corn in its growing and ripening; and during the winter of 1915–16, *Winesburg, Ohio* came to fruition in roughly three growth spurts, with one story often providing the germ for the next, and none needing more than local revision. According to William L. Phillip's ingenious study of the manuscripts, Anderson apparently turned over piles of numbered pages from discarded projects and filled these versos in reverse numerical sequence.[32] Thus, it is possible to determine that the order of composition among the earliest stories was as follows:

1. "The Book of the Grotesque"	7. "Godliness," part III
2. "Hands"	8. "Nobody Knows"
3. "Paper Pills"	9. "Respectability"
4. "Tandy"	10. "The Thinker"
5. "Drink"	11. "Godliness," part IV
6. "Mother"	

The writing of the first two parts of "Godliness" followed after an interval; then came a third harvest of stories, some probably dashed off during slow days at the advertising office: "Adventure," "The Strength of God," "The Teacher," "Loneliness," "An Awakening." The concluding three – "Death," "Sophistication," and "Departure" – were evidently composed months later as Anderson prepared *Winesburg* for book publication by fleshing out the character and experience of George Willard.[33] Although he thought retrospectively that the stories, taken together, "made something like a novel" about a boy growing into manhood,[34] it is doubtful that Anderson held such a conception of the book from the outset.

In any case, *Winesburg, Ohio* is neither a novel nor a random set of stories. Rather it is one of the earliest examples of an important American genre, as yet unnamed by literary historians, that comprises such works as Sarah Orne Jewett's *The Country of the Pointed Firs* (1896), Jean Toomer's *Cane* (1923), Ernest Hemingway's *In Our Time* (1925), William Faulkner's *Go Down, Moses* (1942), and

John Steinbeck's *The Red Pony* (1945). These and other books in the genre are collections of short fictions, often centered on a recurring character, that work synergistically, adding up to more than the sum of their parts despite their lacking the narrative coherence of a novel. Nevertheless, as Marcia Jacobson and Clare Colquitt suggest (later in this volume), *Winesburg, Ohio* may also be related to the traditions of the American boy book, the *Bildungs-roman*, and the *Künstlerroman*. Its derivation from specific literary sources is more difficult to trace because Anderson's memories of what he had read were often erratic and misleading. Reviewers and critics, however, have pointed out affinities to James Joyce's *Dubliners* (1914), which Anderson claimed not to have encountered before writing *Winesburg*, and to Ivan Turgenev's *A Sportsman's Sketches* (1847–51), which he definitely *had* read. Closer to home were the depictions of small-town America in Masters's *Spoon River Anthology*, the undoubted influence of which Anderson took pains to deny,[35] and in the New England poems of E. A. Robinson and Robert Frost, especially *North of Boston* (1915).

Frost was one member of the advisory board of the *Seven Arts*, a New York little magazine that became Anderson's vehicle to the larger literary world after his Chicago circle dispersed. By 1915, Floyd Dell had already moved to New York to co-edit the *Masses*, where three of the Winesburg stories appeared in 1916 (before the last of them had been written): "The Book of the Grotesque" (February), "Hands" (March), and "The Strength of God" (August). But when the editors' enthusiasm for Anderson waned, he was left with no outlet except the *Little Review* in Chicago, which printed "Paper Pills" (under the title, "The Philosopher") in March 1917 and "An Awakening" in December 1918. Fortuitously, Anderson was put in contact with Waldo Frank, co-editor of the *Seven Arts*, with whom he exchanged confiding letters throughout the winter of 1915–16. Frank and others connected to the *Seven Arts*, notably Van Wyck Brooks and Paul Rosenfeld, were captivated by the stories Anderson began to submit, four of which were published: "Queer" (December 1916), "The Untold Lie" (January 1917), "Mother" (March 1917), and "The Thinker" (September 1917). During the summer of 1916, Anderson and Tennessee Mitchell (whom he was about to marry) invited Frank to join them at Lake Chateaugay in upstate New York. The two men became close (but not lasting) friends, and early the next year Anderson finally paid a visit to the *Seven Arts* office in New York.

This literary pilgrimage recalls Howells's famous journey to Boston in 1860 to seek affiliation to the elders of New England literature. To Emerson, Hawthorne, Lowell, and Holmes the young Ohioan represented the rising West and the future hope of American literature. By initiating him into their "apostolic succession," they made Howells heir to New England culture itself.[36] Anderson, too, had arisen in Ohio, and he was embraced (as well as subtly patronized) by the New Yorkers as an unpolished prophet of a western America as yet unconstrained by eastern cultural refinement. But, unlike Howells, Anderson was not lighting his torch at the eastern shrine; he was returning the flame. Already an elder in years, he stood paradoxically for what Brooks called in 1915 "America's Coming-of-Age." Speaking for the "younger generation," Brooks outlined the dilemma from which Anderson's work promised an escape:

> Our disbelief in experience, our habitual repression of the creative instinct, our consequent over-stimulation of the acquisitive instinct, has made it impossible for us to take advantage of the treasures our own life has yielded. . .
>
> A new age has begun, an age of intensive cultivation, and it is the creative life that the nation calls for now. But for that how ill-equipped we are! Our literature has prepared no pathways for us, our leaders are themselves lost.[37]

As a potential leader, Anderson was singularly qualified by his having repressed not his creative but his acquisitive instinct. For the *Seven Arts* group, he was an honorary member of the "younger generation," all the more honorable for being truly of the generation they were rejecting. Anderson, that is, became a cultural commodity; as author, he was assigned a particular exchange value within the literary economy, one largely (but not entirely) determined by the rebellious new entrepreneurs of American letters, those like Frank and Brooks who were outspoken advocates of artistic renewal.

The "Anderson" constructed by his champions at the *Seven Arts* was also the one recognized, both positively and negatively, by the first reviews of *Winesburg, Ohio*. On the whole they were favorable, even from unexpected quarters. In the *New York Times*, for example, William Lyon Phelps, a popular Yale professor and a voice of the eastern establishment, related Anderson's art to the ideas of Freud and Jung: "Conceivably these stories might have been written before the advent of the new psychology, but if so they would not have been understood." For Phelps, Anderson was unmistakably a modern writer, one gifted with an "extraordinary quality of vividness, sincerity, tenderness."[38] The conservative *Boston Transcript* likewise admired the "genius" of "tales so simple on the surface, so deep beneath the surface, so clear in their mirroring of the truths in human nature that have turned character and experience into the grotesques of realism." Anderson gave proof "of what American fiction can be when an artist with vision and sensibility, with comprehension and the capacity to test reality with imagination, deals with the infinities that lie beneath the commonplace materials of American life."[39]

Among reviewers from the younger generation, the poet Hart Crane was the most ecstatic, proclaiming that "America should read this book on her knees. It constitutes an important chapter in the Bible of her consciousness."[40] H. L. Mencken, perhaps the chief arbiter of modern taste in 1919, was scarcely less enthusiastic in asserting that *Winesburg, Ohio* was "of a new order" and that Anderson belonged to "a small group that has somehow emancipated itself from the prevailing imitativeness and banality of the national letters." Indeed, Anderson achieved the goal that *Spoon River Anthology* had "aimed at, and missed by half a mile." *Winesburg*, Mencken declared, was "a truly extraordinary book, by a man of such palpably unusual talent that it seems almost an impertinence to welcome him."[41]

Comparisons to Masters, usually to Anderson's advantage, abounded in the reviews, as did allusions to the revered Russians, Leo Tolstoy, Fyodor Dostoyevsky, and Anton Chekhov, none of whom Anderson had actually read by 1919. The implicit purpose of such measurements was to establish Anderson as an American writer worthy to stand beside the canonized European masters and simultaneously to cut the Europeans down to size by impugning the literary patriotism of their American adherents. As Burton

Rascoe alleged:

> Unquestionably, Mr. Anderson's book will offend a great number of
> readers, many of whom are quite willing to admit that Chekhov and
> Dostoievski, being Russians, are great and significant writers. These
> people, too, it is likely, are among the numerous disparagers of our
> native literature who frequently ask why America does not produce
> writers of the caliber to be found abroad. The answer is that for the
> most part America does, and in far greater numbers than the read-
> ing public is entitled to; for the closer an American approximates
> the literary excellence of Europe, the more shameless is the native
> neglect of him.[42]

The charge of "native neglect" is as old as the attempt to free
American literature from European domination, as old, that is, as
"American literature" itself, which came into being through the
arguments of apologists and critics in the early nineteenth century.
If, as Brooks and others thought, the blooming of a new American
literature in the early years of the twentieth century was equivalent to the literary flowering of a century before, then Anderson
was a counterpart to writers like Irving, Cooper, and Hawthorne,
whose reliance on commonplace American materials was one
gauge of their "caliber," one sign of their "literary excellence." But
modernist literary history, as invented by Brooks's generation, also
stressed the idea that authentic native genius had continually been
crippled because it had been forced into an adversarial posture
toward the prevailing values of middle-class American society. The
narrative of stifled creativity that informed Brooks's influential histories of American literature seemed to explain the frustrated career of Mark Twain, for example, or of Melville, who was rescued
from obscurity during the 1920s and refashioned into a "contemporary."

The challenge for true contemporaries was somehow to retain
the integrity that modernist critics attributed to those in opposition
to American bourgeois culture and still to triumph artistically. This
was the challenge that Anderson was deemed to have met. The
initial success of *Winesburg, Ohio* depended, then, not only on its
imaginative qualities but also on the perception of its author as an
iconoclast and muckraker. Despite his evident sympathy for the
grotesques, he was seen to be exposing the scandal of their repres-

sion and vacuity. Most of the reviewers in Chicago, who puffed Anderson as a native son, urbanely affirmed the typicality of Winesburg: a midwestern village as oppressive as the ones they too had fled, against which any respectable modern would revolt.

The truthfulness of Anderson's vision to which his followers attested was questioned, however, by those who deplored what one (positive) reviewer called his frank treatment of "sex repression and sex outbursts."[43] Complaining that *Winesburg* had reduced "human clay" to "plain dirt," the *New York Sun* could recommend the book only to readers seeking "a sort of handy guide to all of the Spoon Rivers – wherein obscenity, insanity, vain pomp and hardness of heart are expatiated upon, and they can wallow in perversion and abnormality to their souls' content."[44] Another reader protested the favorable review of *Winesburg* in the *Chicago Daily News:* "If such stuff makes the great American novel we have that precious volume already in the latest report of the psychopathic hospital, and the history of the world has for its author Dr. P. von Kraft-Ebing [*sic*]." *Winesburg,* in this view, was less a book of the grotesque than a grotesque book: "Always it returns to a decadent exposure of strange neurotics and the search for the wen and wart on the face of humanity."[45]

By invoking the notoriety of Richard von Krafft-Ebing, the Austrian forensic psychiatrist whose *Psychopathia Sexualis* (1886), a compendium of case histories of "abnormal" sexuality that had shocked readers outside the medical audience for which it was intended, this critic meant to brand the "new psychology" as "decadent" – an exact inversion of Phelps's praise for Freud and Jung, whose ideas were welcomed by the avant-garde in the 1920s as a liberating extension of Krafft-Ebing's work. Although Anderson used the term "neurotic" only once in *Winesburg, Ohio* – and in a context that makes it unclear if he intended a narrowly psychoanalytic meaning[46] – he was inevitably allied to Freud, Jung, and Krafft-Ebing because the "new psychology" and the "new literature" were conflated in the minds of American readers. The best evidence of the text's "modernity," to friends and foes alike, was its seeming to evince this linkage. Whereas in the negative reviews *Winesburg* was tarred with the same brush as was psychoanalysis by those who resisted what was "modern" in both,[47] in the positive reviews Anderson became a "Freudian" despite himself. Hailed, as Frederick Hoffman says, as "the one American writer who knew his psychology and possessed a rich fund of knowledge and experience to which it could best be applied," Anderson nevertheless denied "having actually read Freud or exploited him in his writing" – this despite the vogue of "psyching" among the artists with whom he had mingled in Chicago. In fact, as the psychologist Trigant Burrow testified, Anderson was hostile to the claim that psychoanalysis could "scientifically" cure what he considered to be ineradicable in human nature.[48]

Ironically, Anderson's literary reputation was founded on apparent misapprehensions – that he was the "American Freudian," that he was in "revolt from the village" – and the subsequent history of that reputation is one of successive "misreadings" that Anderson's academic advocates are always trying to correct. As Walter B. Rideout remarks, the fluctuations in critical attitudes toward Anderson "constitute a kind of Rorschach test exhibiting the cultural temper of the successive decades":

> In the 1910's Anderson was frequently rebuked or attacked by the "Establishment" critics and reviewers and almost always praised by the rebellious new ones for his probing of the human psyche and his willingness to reveal what he found there. In the twenties his genuine innovations in the American short story were often perceived in themselves but were more often linked to, or confused with, the personal legend of his abandonment of business for literature. In the thirties – in fact, the repudiation had begun in the late twenties – he was dismissed as a confused man of failing talent who could not comprehend or cope with contemporary social reality. In the forties the writing was rejected as technically deficient, the man as intellectually deficient. In the fifties – again the process had begun in the last years of the previous decade – he was considered worth re-examination, if only as a neglected literary ancestor of the moderns. Finally, in the sixties re-examination became revaluation in the hopes of achieving a balanced understanding of the man, of his work, of his relation to his times, of his exact part in the development of twentieth-century American fiction.[49]

In the two decades since Rideout's summary, little has changed. The impetus for a "balanced understanding," in which the full range of Anderson's work would be reconsidered, reached a climax about the time of his centenary in 1976. By 1981, David D. Anderson could point proudly to a growing body of primary scholarship and sympathetic criticism aimed at transcending the paradox by which Anderson had been relegated "to a minor position in American literary history" by those who nevertheless "are not only unable to ignore him but give him more attention – in some cases much more attention – than many writers they consider to be more significant." This broad revaluation has purportedly gone far toward reversing the all too common assumption that "Anderson's publication of *Winesburg, Ohio* was essentially an aberration, a minor accomplishment in a career that had promised much but remained undistinguished."[50]

From the time of its publication to the present, however, *Winesburg, Ohio* has set the terms for any discussion of Anderson's literary merits – mainly because it has served so long as an indispensable point of reference for orthodox histories of American modernism. *Winesburg*, indeed, is the proof text for the rise of Sherwood Anderson, whose legend has been crucial to distinguishing American modernism from what is thought to have gone before. Just as it is difficult to imagine *Cane, In Our Time*, or *Go Down, Moses* without *Winesburg, Ohio* in the foreground – to cite works by writers who were grateful, at least at first, for Anderson's mentoring example[51] – so it is probable that as long as Toomer, Hemingway, and Faulkner remain central to the canon, so will Anderson, no matter how "minor" a role he may be assigned.

It would require a shift in our literary-historical perspective to create the possibility of Anderson's appearing other than he has thus far been seen. One purpose of the essays that follow is to advance such a revisioning by providing new contexts for *Winesburg, Ohio*. By comparing Anderson's artistic practices not only to those of Gertrude Stein but also to those of some important painters, David Stouck places *Winesburg* within expressionism, a movement that differs subtly but significantly from modernism. Marcia Jacobson treats *Winesburg* as both a *Künstlerroman* and an autobiographical fiction in which Anderson drew on some of the conventions of the American boy book. For Clare Colquitt, the pertinent comparison is to Sarah Orne Jewett and other women writers of "narratives of community." The dislocation of such community is one theme of Thomas Yingling's materialist reading, which brings out the social implications of a text more usually read from a psychological angle. The trajectory of these essays is toward an Anderson who is increasingly defamiliarized: the modernist artist-hero whose legend I have traced becomes a writer at once more and less "modern."

Whatever Sherwood Anderson's future position within (or without) the canon of American literature, it seems unlikely that *Winesburg, Ohio* will easily be displaced from the center of critical interest. The qualities in Anderson that made him seem "altogether young" and that placed him among Brooks's younger generation are also those that may keep *Winesburg,* a book aged seventy-one this year, green in its appeal to younger readers and to the spirit of renewal in older ones.

NOTES

1. Sherwood Anderson, *Winesburg, Ohio,* ed. Malcolm Cowley (New York: Viking Press, 1960), p. 22. All further quotations are taken from this standard edition and are documented in the text.
2. *Letters of Sherwood Anderson,* ed. Howard Mumford Jones and Walter B. Rideout (Boston: Little, Brown, 1953), p. 53.
3. Lionel Trilling, for instance, asserts that "an adolescence must not continue beyond its natural term, and as we read through Anderson's canon what exasperates us is his stubborn, satisfied continuance in his earliest attitudes": *The Liberal Imagination* (New York: Viking Press, 1950; reprinted New York: Anchor Books, 1953), p. 23. Trilling's depreciatory essay, first published after Anderson's death in 1941, marked a watershed in his literary reputation.
4. *Letters to Bab: Sherwood Anderson to Marietta D. Finley, 1916–33,* ed. William A. Sutton (Urbana: University of Illinois Press, 1985), pp. 15–16, 27.
5. *Sherwood Anderson: Selected Letters,* ed. Charles E. Modlin (Knoxville: University of Tennessee Press, 1984), p. 10.
6. *The Rise of Silas Lapham,* ed. Walter J. Meserve and David J. Nordloh (Bloomington: Indiana University Press, 1971), p. 3.
7. Ibid., p. 5.
8. Ibid.

9. Although Anderson had little sympathy for Howells's brand of realism, he read his work attentively; and *Tar: A Midwest Childhood* (1926), a fictionalized account of Anderson's Ohio boyhood, recalls Howells's similar book, *A Boy's Town* (1890).

10. See Howells, "The Man of Letters as a Man of Business" (1893), in *Literature and Life* (New York: Harper, 1902). This important essay on the changing conditions of the literary marketplace and changing status of the American writer at the turn of the twentieth century is pertinent to Anderson's idea of himself as artist.

11. Van Wyck Brooks, *Days of the Phoenix* (New York: Dutton, 1957), p. 31.

12. Kim Townsend, *Sherwood Anderson* (Boston: Houghton Mifflin, 1987), p. 65.

13. Sigmund Freud, "The Most Prevalent Form of Degradation in Erotic Life" (1912), in *Collected Papers*, ed. Joan Riviere (New York: Basic Books, 1959), Vol. 4, pp. 204, 207.

14. Sherwood Anderson, *A Story Teller's Story: A Critical Text*, ed. Ray Lewis White (Cleveland: Case Western Reserve University Press, 1968), p. 65.

15. "Men That Are Wanted," *Agricultural Advertising* 10 (December 1903): 51; quoted in Townsend, *Sherwood Anderson*, p. 48.

16. Anderson, *A Story Teller's Story*, p. 226.

17. *Sherwood Anderson's Memoirs*, ed. Paul Rosenfeld (New York: Harcourt, Brace, 1942), p. 194.

18. "The term that comes closest to describing Anderson's condition is 'fugue state,' a state of flight, something like those Anderson had experienced as a youth when parts of his body, or the landscape, or his very life, seemed to float away." Townsend, *Sherwood Anderson*, p. 81. On Anderson's breakdown, see also William A. Sutton, *The Road to Winesburg: A Mosaic of the Imaginative Life of Sherwood Anderson* (Metuchen, N.J.: Scarecrow Press, 1972), pp. 162–205.

19. Edgar Lee Masters, *Across Spoon River: An Autobiography* (New York: Farrar & Rinehart, 1936), p. 338. For richly detailed background, see Kenny J. Williams, *A Storyteller and a City: Sherwood Anderson's Chicago* (Dekalb: Northern Illinois University Press, 1988).

20. Walter B. Rideout, "Talbot Whittingham and Anderson: A Passage to *Winesburg, Ohio*," in *Sherwood Anderson: Dimensions of His Literary Art*, ed. David D. Anderson (East Lansing: Michigan State University Press, 1976), p. 49.

21. Ibid., p. 54.

22. Sutton, ed., *Letters to Bab*, p. 50.

23. Rosenfeld, ed., *Sherwood Anderson's Memoirs,* pp. 287–8.
24. See William L. Phillips, "How Sherwood Anderson Wrote *Winesburg, Ohio,*" *American Literature* 23 (March 1951): 7–30.
25. Peter G. Filene, *Him/Her/Self: Sex Roles in Modern America,* 2nd ed. (Baltimore: Johns Hopkins University Press, 1986), p. 71.
26. "I wish to preach, not the doctrine of ignoble ease, but the doctrine of the strenuous life, the life of toil and effort, of labor and strife; to preach that highest form of success which comes, not to the man who desires mere easy peace, but to the man who does not shrink from danger, from hardship, or from bitter toil, and who out of these wins the splendid ultimate triumph." "The Strenuous Life" (1900), in *The Works of Theodore Roosevelt* (New York: Scribner, 1926), Vol. 13, p. 319.
27. Townsend, *Sherwood Anderson,* pp. 24, 106–7.
28. "A Part of Earth," in *The Sherwood Anderson Reader,* ed. Paul Rosenfeld (Boston: Houghton Mifflin, 1947), p. 325.
29. Ibid., p. 327.
30. Edward Dahlberg, "My Friends Stieglitz, Anderson, and Dreiser," in *The Edward Dahlberg Reader,* ed. Paul Carroll (Norfolk, Ct.: New Directions, 1967), p. 231.
31. Jones and Rideout, eds., *Letters of Sherwood Anderson,* p. 21.
32. Phillips, "How Sherwood Anderson Wrote *Winesburg, Ohio,*" pp. 10–13.
33. Chastened by the poor sales of *Windy McPherson's Son, Marching Men,* and *Mid-American Chants,* John Lane may have been predisposed to his judgment of the Winesburg stories as too gloomy to attract a large readership. When Lane showed reluctance to publish them as a book, Anderson turned to Ben Huebsch, known for his commitment to innovative work. (He was, for instance, the American publisher of James Joyce and D. H. Lawrence.) *Winesburg, Ohio* – its title suggested by Huebsch in lieu of Anderson's "The Book of the Grotesque" – first appeared in May 1919, in an edition of about 1,800 copies. Contrary to Lane's expectations, it did fairly well. Reprinted four times within the next three years, *Winesburg* reached total sales in the first two years of about 3,000 copies. See William L. Phillips, "The Editions of *Winesburg, Ohio,*" in *Sherwood Anderson: Centennial Studies,* ed. Hilbert H. Campbell and Charles E. Modlin (Troy, N.Y.: Whitson, 1976), pp. 151–5.
34. Rosenfeld, ed., *Sherwood Anderson's Memoirs,* p. 289. In 1938, when he was having trouble with a novel he was writing, Anderson "decided to go back to the *Winesburg* form. That is really a novel. It is a form

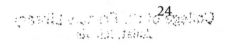

in which I feel at ease. I invented it. It was mine. 'Why not use it,' I told myself." Modlin, ed., *Sherwood Anderson: Selected Letters*, p. 220.

35. "When the reviewers of *Winesburg, Ohio* in 1919 made the obvious comparison between the two books, Anderson's publishers replied with an announcement that 'Mr. Anderson's "Winesburg" stories appeared in magazines before Mr. Masters's work appeared,' clearly a misstatement of the facts." Phillips, "How Sherwood Anderson Wrote *Winesburg, Ohio*," p. 16. Phillips adduces evidence that Anderson had read *Spoon River* early in 1915. His failure to acknowledge Masters's influence may well have been motivated by his devotion to Tennessee Mitchell, who had been Masters's mistress some years before she became Anderson's second wife. Masters was to paint a slanderous portrait of her, albeit disguised by a pseudonym, in *Across Spoon River*.

36. See W. D. Howells, *Literary Friends and Acquaintance* (1900), ed. David F. Hiatt and Edwin H. Cady (Bloomington: Indiana University Press, 1968), p. 36.

37. Van Wyck Brooks, *Three Essays on America* (New York: Dutton, 1934), pp. 147–8. The quoted passage is from "Letters and Leadership" (1918), which Anderson himself approvingly reviewed.

38. William Lyon Phelps, "Winesburg, Ohio," *New York Times Book Review* 29 (June 1919), reprinted in *The Merrill Studies in Winesburg, Ohio*, ed. Ray Lewis White (Columbus, Ohio: Merrill, 1971), pp. 37–9.

39. W.S.B., "Ohio Small Town Life: Commonplace People and Their Everyday Existence," *Boston Transcript*, 11 June 1919, reprinted in White, ed., *Merrill Studies*, pp. 31–3.

40. Hart Crane, review of *Winesburg, Ohio*, *Pagan* 4 (September 1919): 60–1, quoted in Townsend, *Sherwood Anderson*, p. 157.

41. H. L. Mencken, "Something New Under the Sun," *The Smart Set* 59 (August 1919), reprinted in White, ed., *Merrill Studies*, pp. 39–40.

42. Burton Rascoe, "Winesburg, Ohio," *Chicago Tribune*, 7 June 1919, reprinted in White, ed., *Merrill Studies*, pp. 27–30.

43. Llewellyn Jones, "The Unroofing of Winesburg: Tales of Life That Seem Overheard Rather Than Written," *Chicago Evening Post*, 20 June 1919, reprinted in White, ed., *Merrill Studies*, pp. 32–4.

44. "A Gutter Would Be Spoon River," *New York Sun*, 1 June 1919, reprinted in White, ed., *Merrill Studies*, pp. 26–7.

45. Wallace Smith, "Civilian Communique," *Chicago Daily News*, 3 September 1919, quoted in Sutton, *The Road to Winesburg*, pp. 604–6.

46. The passage appears near the beginning of "Surrender" ("Godliness," part III): "Born of a delicate and overworked mother, and an im-

pulsive, hard, imaginative father, who did not look with favor upon
her coming into the world, Louise [Bentley] was from childhood a
neurotic, one of the race of over-sensitive women that in later days
industrialism was to bring in such great numbers into the world" (p.
87). In its pre-Freudian usage, "neurotic" referred broadly to diseases
of the nervous system, including the "nervous prostrations" that became so common in the later nineteenth century, especially among
women.

47. See, for example, H. W. Boynton's review: "At worst he seems in this
book like a man who has too freely imbibed the doctrine of the
psychoanalysts, and fares thereafter with eyes slightly 'set' along the
path of fiction." "All Over the Lot," *Bookman* 49 (1919): 729.

48. Frederick J. Hoffman, *Freudianism and the Literary Mind*, 2nd ed.
(Baton Rouge: Louisiana State University Press, 1957), pp. 229, 235–
6. After an exhaustive examination of the evidence, Hoffman concludes that although Anderson's interests ran parallel to Freud's –
both were concerned with dreams, for example – he was not deeply
and directly influenced by psychoanalysis.

49. Walter B. Rideout, "Sherwood Anderson," in *Fifteen Modern American
Authors: A Survey of Research and Criticism*, ed. Jackson R. Bryer (Durham, N.C.: Duke University Press, 1969), p. 11.

50. David D. Anderson, "Sherwood Anderson and the Critics," in *Critical
Essays on Sherwood Anderson*, ed. David D. Anderson (Boston: G. K.
Hall, 1981), pp. 4, 6.

51. On Anderson's relationships with Hemingway and Faulkner, both of
whom more or less repudiated the man who had served them so well
at the start of their careers, see William L. Phillips, "Sherwood Anderson's Two Prize Pupils," in *The Achievement of Sherwood Anderson:
Essays in Criticism*, ed. Ray Lewis White (Chapel Hill: University of
North Carolina Press, 1966), pp. 202–10. On Anderson and Toomer,
see Darwin T. Turner, "An Intersection of Paths: Correspondence Between Jean Toomer and Sherwood Anderson," and Mark Helbling,
"Sherwood Anderson and Jean Toomer," both in *Jean Toomer: A Critical Evaluation*, ed. Therman B. O'Daniel (Washington, D.C.: Howard
University Press, 1988).

2

Anderson's Expressionist Art

DAVID STOUCK

IN the introductory sketch in *Winesburg, Ohio* the narrator tries to describe what is inside an old writer as he lies on his high bed. Is it a baby, a youth, a young woman wearing a coat of mail like a knight? He cannot say (p. 22). In the first story, "Hands," the narrator is again reflecting on what is concealed from sight: "Let us look briefly into the story of the hands. Perhaps our talking of them will arouse the poet who will tell the hidden wonder story" (p. 31). And in the following piece, "Paper Pills," we are told that "Winesburg had forgotten the old man, but in Doctor Reefy there were the seeds of something very fine" (p. 35). Each passage makes reference to human potential that has not yet been uncovered and released.

In the third story, "Mother," we are introduced to Elizabeth Willard, a woman who is withdrawn and silent, especially in her relation to her husband. But with her son George, a young newspaper reporter, she has established a deep bond of sympathy that centers on her desire that he do something with his life that will justify her unhappy existence. She prays to God, saying she will take any blow he might inflict "if but this my boy be allowed to express something for us both" (p. 40). She prays, in effect, to be released through her son from her lonely isolation. Elizabeth Willard's prayer is important because it describes the motive behind the Winesburg stories: the artist's desire "to express something" for his characters, to break down barriers and release them from their frustration and loneliness. Equally important is the phrasing of the mother's prayer, "to express something for us both," because it suggests the formal approach Anderson took to his writing, an approach best described by the term "expressionism."

In essays and letters, Anderson stated repeatedly that the goal of his writing was to bring to the surface the hidden depths of thought and feeling in the characters he created, characters representing ordinary humanity in the America of his time. In a particularly vivid statement of these intentions, he wrote to his publisher, Ben Huebsch, that "there is within every human being a deep well of thinking over which a heavy iron lid is kept clamped." The artist's task was to tear that lid away so that "a kind of release takes place" that "cuts sharply across all the machinery of the life about him."[1] His method was to write stories that were almost plotless in the conventional sense, stories that focused instead on an intense moment of feeling. He said in *The "Writer's Book"* that a "short story is the result of a sudden passionate interest,"[2] and to Huebsch he wrote that it often would come "all at one sitting, a distillation, an outbreak."[3] That quality of a sudden insight, a revelation, an "outbreak" is what is most indelible in the Winesburg fictions – a repressed woman running naked out onto the lawn in the rain, a minister waving a bloodied fist in the air after breaking the window in the church study. The Winesburg stories accumulate power from those exaggerated, stylized gestures by which a character is revealed or through which a scream of suffering is made to be heard. "Expressionism" is the formal term especially suitable to describing Anderson's art, because in common with the dramatists and painters in that period, Anderson made it his goal to give outward expression to the intense private feelings of both the artist and the characters he created.

1

The link between Anderson and painting is important; he often described himself as a painter using the medium of words. He saw both painter and writer trying, above all else, to express human emotions. Anderson enjoyed a lifelong association with a number of painters. His older brother, Karl, with whom he was always closely associated, made his living as a portrait painter in New York; Karl was involved in bringing a portion of the famous Armory Show to Chicago's Art Institute in 1913. His second wife, Tennessee Mitchell, worked as a sculptor, and Anderson himself turned to the canvas on several occasions to express the essence of what he was experiencing. But probably more important for his writing was his friendship with Alfred Stieglitz, the photographer and art enthusiast, whose gallery "291" introduced Anderson to the best experimental painting being done in America at that time. Anderson was taken to the gallery by Paul Rosenfeld as early as 1917 (he was then writing the later Winesburg stories and had come East to meet the editor of the *Seven Arts* who was publishing them).[4] At the gallery he saw works by Marsden Hartley, John Marin, Arthur Dove, and Georgia O'Keeffe. Through Stieglitz he came to know these artists personally and commented in letters and notebooks on their work. In *A Story Teller's Story* he states that seeing the work of these modern painters "had given me a new feeling for form and color."[5]

What these painters revealed to Anderson was that representational accuracy conveyed only life's surfaces, that an artist, whether painter or writer, had to alter the perception of surface reality so that "the hidden inner truth" of the subject would emerge. In "A Note on Realism," he refers to Marin's Brooklyn Bridge paintings as examples of art being very different from reality.[6] Marin's paintings of the bridge are not photographic, but transcribe through expressionistic distortions and tiltings the hidden dynamic forces the painter felt present in all things, even man-made engineering structures. Anderson admitted a special preference for the nature paintings of Arthur Dove: "Perhaps at bottom I'm like Dove, a country man. The warm earth feeling gets me hardest."[7] Typically, Dove's paintings render the rural environment, including its flora and fauna, in a stylized way. His country landscapes are not suggestive of a visionary mystery or symbolism, but present nature as vibrantly alive, physically immanent. In his collection of critical essays titled *Port of New York*, which includes an essay on Anderson, Paul Rosenfeld writes of Dove's work in a way that describes Anderson's often stated intentions: Dove's painting of grazing cows "brings the knowledge of someone who has almost gotten into the kine themselves; and felt from within the rich animality of their being . . . and then given it out again in characteristic abstraction."[8]

Through Stieglitz, Anderson also came to know the work of

Gertrude Stein. Anderson's first exposure to Stein is presumed to have been the August 1912 copy of Stieglitz's *Camera Work*, which contained Stein's experimental pieces "Henri Matisse" and "Pablo Picasso."[9] It is in the correspondence between Stein and Anderson and in his published writings about her that Anderson most fully discusses his writing in terms of painting. Although the friendship with Stein began after the publication of *Winesburg, Ohio*, his writing about her contains summary opinions held since first reading her work. In *A Story Teller's Story*, dedicated to Stieglitz, he describes his excitement when first reading her purely experimental prose; it reminded him of when he had once been taken into a painter's studio to be shown the painter's colors. In Stein's writing, words were separated from sense: "Here were words laid before me as the painter had laid the color pans on the table in my presence." It struck him then that "words used by the tale teller were as the colors used by the painter."[10] In a later piece about Stein, defending her against the charge of automatic writing, he observes that "word is laid against word as carefully and always instinctively as any painter would lay one color against another."[11] In her review of *A Story Teller's Story*, she pays her admirer a compliment by saying that his book does not reflect, describe, embroider, or photograph life, but expresses it "and to express life takes essential intelligence."[12] And after *Sherwood Anderson's Notebook* was published in 1926, with its chapter on the young William Faulkner, she wrote to him suggesting that he should someday "write a novel that is just one portrait,"[13] comparing his writing to the work of a painter.

Anderson was complimented indeed by Stein's review of his work, because when she said that he had succeeded in expressing life rather than merely describing it, she was including him with the modern artists whom he so much admired. The verb Stein chose was increasingly being used to describe the artistic goal of the avant-garde. The term "expressionism," however loosely applied, indicated the artist's rejection of a surface realism and the attempt instead to make mainfest the hidden essence of things. It was an attempt, in Freudian terms, to reveal the secret inner life. "What Expressionist art seeks to render visible," writes Ulrich Weisstein, "are soul states and the violent emotions welling up from the innermost recesses of the subconscious."[14] The things that are caught on canvas or on the page are the extreme moods, such as fear, despair, or ecstasy, but it is especially the soul in anguish that the expressionist desires to project – Edvard Munch's painting, *The Scream* being a classic example. Anderson, in a letter to Marietta D. Finley, describes himself working on the Winesburg stories with the same goal: "My mind is tumbling about and trying to fit itself in a mood of sustained work. That will come. You must of course know that the things you want, the warm close thing, is the cry going up out of all hearts."[15]

Critics have acknowledged that the term "realism" does not accurately describe Anderson's writing. Walter B. Rideout has written that "what Anderson is after is less a representation of 'reality' than, to [draw] a metaphor from art, an abstraction of it." He goes on to point out that in Anderson's stories, "what is important is 'to see beneath the surface of lives,' to perceive the intricate mesh of impulses, desires, drives growing deep down in the dark, unrevealed parts of the personality."[16] Similarly, Irving Howe observes that "Anderson is not trying to represent . . . the immediate surface of human experience; he is rather drawing the abstract and deliberately distorted paradigm of an extreme situation."[17] Expressionist art cannot, strictly speaking, be designated abstract, because it remains referential, content-oriented, but it does reject the methods of verisimilitude in favor of more stylized techniques – distortions (in both art and literature) of color, shape, syntax, vocabulary, oversimplification of form, exaggeration. The grotesque is often the result of these distortions. Anderson's art in *Winesburg, Ohio* is a particularly striking example of expressionism in literature, where the narrative yields repeatedly to a violent projection outward of "soul states" or, as Howe phrases it, "conditions of psychic deformity."[18]

Short stories are especially congenial to expressionist art, because plot (cause and effect) is pared down to its simplest form. Action in expressionist fiction is always secondary to the transmission of an inner feeling or vision of the world. For example, in *Three Lives*, Stein was concerned to "express" what she referred to as the ground nature of her characters, the essence of the personality, and was not very interested in what happened to them in their daily lives except as it manifested something of the inner life. Similarly, O'Neill's expressionist plays, such as *The Hairy Ape* and *The Emperor Jones*, consist of a few characters and a series of short scenes that dramatize vividly his vision of human nature and society's ills. In longer dramatic narratives, action becomes more important, and fully rounded characters acquire more psychological particularity, which works against the purpose of expressionist art.

But expressionism is more than a style; it is a *Weltanschauung*. Historically it was a reaction in the early twentieth century against the increasing mechanization of society. The impact of the Industrial Revolution in Western civilization was permeating all aspects of living, from the nature of one's work to the forms of one's recreation. In the American Midwest, Sherwood Anderson witnessed the transition of the small town from a rural economy to a factory-based economy. The loss he most lamented was the craftsman's relation to the world, a loss he viewed as both material and aesthetic:

> with the coming into general use of machinery men did lose the grip of what is perhaps the most truly important of man's functions in life . . . the right. . . to stand alone in the presence of his tools and his materials and with those tools and materials to attempt to twist, to bend, to form something that will be expression of his inner hunger for the truth that is his own and that is beauty.[19]

Anderson had participated in America's industrial "progress" as both an advertising man and a man with his own business. Accordingly, he knew firsthand how individuals are affected by work on an assembly line, how human relations change in a mechanized and commercial world. He told the story of "progress" in the four-part tale "Godliness" in *Winesburg, Ohio* and in *Poor White*, the novel that followed the tales. In both stories the protagonists become slaves of the machinery they use to acquire wealth; they become frustrated and life-destroying figures. Anderson describes men turning to their machines, especially big cars, to compensate for a kind of physical impotence felt when a man no longer works with his hands, no longer expresses himself by crafting things.

To counter humankind's impotence in the age of the machine, the expressionists turned to the cult of primitivism, celebrating generally, as the Fauvists did specifically, the wild beast in man. It was also an acknowledgment of Freud, who was laying bare the phantasms repressed in the depths of the human psyche. For Anderson, the cult of the primitive was a way of rebelling against the repressive work ethic of Puritanism, the specific legacy of American history. In *A Story Teller's Story*, he describes the artist as "a man with a passion" who "wants to dream of color, to lay hold of form, free the sensual in himself, live more freely and fully in his contact with the materials before him than he can possibly live in life."[20] In *Winesburg, Ohio*, this emerges in the descriptions of men who retain something of the child in their characters (figures such as Enoch Robinson), and in *Dark Laughter* (1925) it emerges in the celebration of the American Negro and African-American culture. Releasing "the hidden passion of people"[21] was Anderson's artistic goal as he created the characters in *Winesburg, Ohio*. At the same time, to make visible the inner passionate life was the program central to the expressionist movement in the arts.

2

In a letter to a Russian translator in 1923, Anderson said that the first two novels he published were written under the influence of his reading rather than from his own reactions to life.[22] Looking at *Windy McPherson's Son* (1916) and *Marching Men* (1917), one thinks indeed of realists like Howells and Dreiser, writers committed to recording the changes taking place in society from a journalistic, and in Dreiser's case pseudo-scientific, perspective. It was with the Winesburg stories that he felt he "had really begun to write out of the repressed, muddled life about [him]."[23] One might well describe the characters and situations in the first two novels as repressed and muddled – the words seem appropriate to the content of all of Anderson's work. However, there is a big change between the first two novels and the short fiction, and it is a radical stylistic change, effected in part by the influence of Gertrude Stein. The style in the Winesburg stories is not the realistic, conventional prose style of the period, but rather a vastly simplified kind of writing in which image, rhythm, and what Anderson calls "word color" stand out sharply as the crucial elements in the writing. This is because Anderson has changed his choices of words and the structuring of his sentences.

A passage from *Windy McPherson's Son* beside one from *Winesburg, Ohio* will reveal the change in style. Each passage describes a man living in a town in the Midwest who is remarkable for his unusual appearance. From *Windy McPherson's Son:*

> At the age of forty-five John Telfer was a tall, slender, fine looking man, with black hair and a little black pointed beard, and with something lazy and care-free in his every movement and impulse. Dressed in white flannels, with white shoes, a jaunty cap upon his head, eyeglasses hanging from a gold chain, and a cane lightly swinging from his hand, he made a figure that might have passed unnoticed on the promenade before some fashionable summer hotel, but that seemed a breach of the laws of nature when seen on the streets of a corn-shipping town in Iowa. And Telfer was aware of the extraordinary figure he cut; it was a part of his programme of life. Now as Sam approached he laid a hand on Freedom Smith's shoulder to check the song, and, with his eyes twinkling with good-humour, began thrusting with his cane at the boy's feet.[24]

From "Paper Pills" in *Winesburg, Ohio:*

> He was an old man with a white beard and huge nose and hands. Long before the time during which we will know him, he was a doctor and drove a jaded white horse from house to house through the streets of Winesburg. Later he married a girl who had money. She had been left a large fertile farm when her father died. The girl was quiet, tall, and dark, and to many people she seemed very beautiful. Everyone in Winesburg wondered why she married the doctor. Within a year after the marriage she died.
>
> The knuckles of the doctor's hands were extraordinarily large. When the hands were closed they looked like clusters of unpainted wooden balls as large as walnuts fastened together by steel rods. He smoked a cob pipe and after his wife's death sat all day in his empty office close by a window that was covered with cobwebs. He never opened the window. Once on a hot day in August he tried but found it stuck fast and after that he forgot all about it. (p. 35)

The differences in these two passages reveal the emergence of Anderson's expressionistic style. The passage from *Windy McPherson's Son* (155 words) consists of four long sentences, three of which are compound-complex in construction. The same number of words from the *Winesburg, Ohio* passage compose ten sentences, four of which are simple, and none of which are compound-complex. The immediate effect of radically simplifying the sentences is to make their content stand out more sharply. Although we are given considerable information about John Telfer in the *McPherson* passage – he is tall, slender, fine-looking, with black hair and pointed beard, and is lazy, carefree, good-humored, and an elegant dresser – the portrait is nonetheless blurred by the arrangement of the details in a series of qualifying phrases. In the second sentence of the *McPherson* passage the details of Telfer's appearance have even less impact because of the delay in identifying the subject ("he") they modify. In the *Winesburg* passage the effect of the shorter sentences with so few subordinate clauses is to render the information about Dr. Reefy with clarity and conciseness. Moreover, there is a rhythm to these short declarative sentences that makes the information solid and incontrovertible, rhetorically unimpeachable statements of fact, not subject to the delays, qualifications, or elaborations in the *McPherson* paragraph.

There is also the difference in point of view. While the *McPherson* passage is propositionally a much denser text, the importance of the information is diminished by being interpreted, evaluated for the reader by an omniscient narrator. We are told that Telfer is fine-looking, but that he appears to be lazy and carefree. We are told that he cuts a strange figure in a corn-shipping town in Iowa. The omniscient narrator also informs us of Telfer's awareness of the impression he creates. The reader is a passive recipient of this information. In the *Winesburg* passage, on the other hand, the lexical items are not interpreted, nor is the staging of the text. The old man (Dr. Reefy) has a white beard, and huge nose and hands, but we are not told if they are attractive or ugly. Nor are we given a source of information for this portrait. The story begins, "He was an old man," presupposing in the use of a pronoun rather than a name that information has preceded. Then the speech situation shifts to "we" and later to "everyone's" point of view. Anderson risks coherence in these shifts in point of view and also in the shifts of subject, from "he" to "she" in the first paragraph to the doctor's hands as subject in paragraph two. This technique foregrounds the art of the story, making us aware of a story being told through many perspectives, rather than a scene being reported as in the

McPherson passage. It is the difference between a formal, written description of characters and events and oral storytelling.

"How fond we both are of sentences," Stein wrote to Anderson, recommending some of her own in *The Making of Americans*.[25] The sentence was a subject they frequently discussed, and it remained central to their concept of what was new and important in their art. In 1929, Stein tells Anderson, "I am working fairly steadily on the sentence . . . I struggled all last year with grammar, vocabulary is easier, and now I think before more grammar I must find out what is the essence of a sentence."[26] And in his defense of Stein in the *Atlantic Monthly* in 1934, Anderson talks about words and sentences as the materials of the craft and says he has "often heard sentences on the street that glow like jewels." In the same essay he praises Hemingway: "The man can make sentences. He is one of the few American writers who can."[27]

Anderson wrote frequently about the power of sentences to reveal the life within:

> There are sentences written by all writers of note in all countries that have their roots deep down in the life about them. The sentences are like windows looking into houses. Something is suddenly torn aside, all lies, all trickery about life, gone for the moment.[28]

The bedrock of simple sentences in Anderson's prose signals a paring down to the basic experiences and thoughts of the character. The essential facts about Dr. Reefy's life are telescoped into just a few short sentences in the passage cited. The repetitive rhythm of those sentences with their coordinating conjunctions allows Anderson to express an element of fatality to the doctor's life. Repetition was more crucial to Stein's delineation of character in *Three Lives*, but Anderson also uses repetition to get at the essential nature of his character. Here the detail of the doctor's huge hands is repeated and exemplified in a grotesque image of hands like clusters of unpainted wooden balls. The other item repeated is the fact of his wife's death. The old man's strange appearance and his isolation are linked by his repetition, which suggests some inner truth about the character.

Anderson also wrote about the power of individual words to reveal the life within, and once again he credits Gertrude Stein with awakening him to the expressionist power of language. He compares first reading Stein somewhere around 1915 to the excitement of exploring a new and wonderful country, a sort of Lewis and Clark expedition:

> Here were words laid before me as the painter had laid the color pans on the table in my presence. My mind did a kind of jerking flop and after Miss Stein's book had come into my hands I spent days going about with a tablet of paper in my pocket and making new and strange combinations of words. The result was I thought a new familiarity with the words of my own vocabulary. . . . Perhaps it was then I really fell in love with words, wanted to give each word I used every chance to show itself at its best.[29]

Anderson was describing the period when he began the Winesburg stories. Stein instilled in Anderson a new respect and love for good solid Anglo-Saxon words from common life. In the preface to *Geography and Plays*, he wrote that "here is one artist who has been able to accept ridicule . . . to go live among the little housekeeping words, the swaggering bullying street-corner words, the honest working, money saving words."[30] And in his essay on Stein in "Four American Impressions" he describes her as a woman in a great kitchen of words, making wonderful preserves from the words of our English speech. In this essay and elsewhere he talks about the sensuality of words. In her kitchen, he writes, Stein "is laying word against word, relating sound to sound, feeling for the taste, the smell, the rhythm of the individual word."[31] It is when words have color and smell, Anderson suggests, that they can convey "the life within."

The paragraphs cited earlier from *Windy McPherson's Son* and *Winesburg, Ohio* again illustrate the way Anderson dramatically sharpened his use of language by the time he wrote the Winesburg tales. Anderson's style was never what might be described as "learned." There is never an abundance of Latinate words in his vocabulary. A marked distinction between the two texts, however, can be seen in the frequent use of vague, unspecific words and phrases in the first passage and uninterpreted, clear, hard, denotative language in the second. Words and phrases like "fine looking," "something lazy and care-free," "might have passed unnoticed," "breach of the laws of nature," and "programme of life" lack specificity. They are suggestive, but not clear or focused in their reference. In the Winesburg passage there are no words or phrases that are comparably vague and suggestive; solid Anglo-Saxon nouns like "horse," "house," "knuckles," and "hands" and adjectives like "huge," "jaded," "large," "tall," "dark," and "empty" are simple and clear in reference. There are no clauses in the conditional mode ("might have passed unnoticed"), no inflated phrases like "a breach of the laws of nature" or "programme of life" that might call for explication. Words that convey simple statements of fact reveal directly the bleak, narrow confines of Dr. Reefy's existence as something innate and inescapable, whereas the unusual character of John Telfer in the first passage is never clearly defined or felt; it is something the reader is told.

"One works with words," wrote Anderson about Stein, "and one would like words that have a perfume to the nostrils, rattling words one can throw into a box and shake, making a sharp, jingling sound, words that, when seen on the printed page, have a distinct arresting effect upon the eye."[32] In the simile describing Dr. Reefy's hands, Anderson releases the physicality of the words used. The doctor's knuckles are like "clusters of unpainted wooden balls as large as walnuts fastened together by steel rods." The words are arresting because of their unusual use in this descriptive context. The words are familiar from farm and workshop ("the little housekeeping words . . . the honest working, money saving words"), but in this context they achieve a curiously poetic quality. The twisted, grotesque character to the doctor's inner life is expressed in a powerfully visible way. As Linda W. Wagner has observed, the emotional life of each character in *Winesburg, Ohio* is presented graphically rather than rhetorically;[33] that is, we are made to see and experience for ourselves the inner life of the character, rather than being told about it.

The result is not realism but expressionism. Reality and art are always separate, Anderson argued, and although realism may be very good journalism, it is always bad art.[34] Anderson was often told that in *Winesburg, Ohio* he had given an exact picture of Ohio village life, but he said that in fact the idea for his characters came from observing his fellow lodgers in a Chicago boardinghouse, not from recalling the villagers of his youth. On other occasions, however, he would credit memories of Clyde, Ohio, as the source of the book. Both statements are probably true and reveal something of his method as an expressionist writer. In his "A Note on Realism" and in his *Memoirs*, Anderson describes his method of creating character. He explains that he would try in his writing to get at "some inner truth" of a character that he had observed, but would then put that character into the physical body of another to see if the essence of the characterization remained intact.[35] Sometimes boardinghouse residents would merge with remembered figures from Clyde. In that way the character would become a denizen of Anderson's imaginative world, no longer an individual realistically observed and drawn "true to life," but a character whose essential being transcended the physical body of the prototype, assuming other external features more expressive of the individual's essential nature.

Another major change in Anderson's writing when he moved from the early novels to the Winesburg stories was a shift away from plot. As an expressionist drama, there is little development of a story line in the Winesburg tales in terms of cause and effect. Typically a story begins with a physical description of the central character, emphasizing some grotesque feature or trait. Then, usually in relation to George Willard as listener, something of the character's past history is revealed (a desertion, a death in the family, an unwanted pregnancy). The story usually ends with the character committing a desperate act (getting drunk, shouting in the streets, striking at the newspaper reporter), then fleeing temporarily from the town. By means of distortion and repetition, rather than plot, Anderson is able to reveal something about the hidden inner life of his characters and about the nature of society.

In Anderson's view, the chief obstacle to exploring fully the world of the imagination was the conventional demand for plot. Refusing to acknowledge the importance of plot in fiction became a point of honor with Anderson. Repeatedly in his writings he blames his lack of commercial success on the fact that he would not craft his stories on the formula of de Maupassant or O. Henry, writers whom he considered slick. In *A Story Teller's Story* he writes heatedly on the subject, distinguishing plot from form:

> There was a notion that ran through all story telling in America,
> that stories must be built about a plot and that absurd Anglo-Saxon
> notion that they must point a moral, uplift the people, make better
> citizens, etc, etc. The magazines were filled with these plot stories
> and most of the plays on our stage were plot plays. "The Poison
> Plot" I called it in conversation with my friends as the plot notion
> did seem to me to poison all story telling. What was wanted I
> thought was form, not plot, an altogether more elusive and difficult
> thing to come at.[36]

True form, he wrote in his defense of Stein, emerges from words
and sentences. Again, drawing an analogy with painting, he wrote
that words have color value, and therein lies true form.[37] Writing
to Paul Rosenfeld in 1921, he said that he would not be bound by
the critic's idea of form, for if he wrapped his packages up more
neatly, he would lose the "large, loose sense of life" he was after.
In the same letter, he added: "One thing I would like you to know
is this: as far as I am concerned, I can accept no standard I have
ever seen as to form. What I most want is to be and remain always
an experimenter, an adventurer."[38] When he was actually writing
the Winesburg stories in 1917, he called them fragments.[39]

This approach is evident in "Tandy," a Winesburg piece with no
plot or story line at all. Three characters appear in the sketch: an
agnostic widower, his daughter, who is still a child, and a red-
haired young man who has come to live in Winesburg and hopes
there to overcome his alcoholism. The only character with a name
is the widower, Tom Hard. He befriends the young stranger, but the
latter does not stop drinking. The only event that takes place is
when the drunken stranger one evening drops to the knees and
tells the little girl to be "Tandy," the quality in a woman of being
"brave enough to dare to be loved" (p. 145). The point of the
sketch is to reveal something that is missing in human relationships – courage for sexual expression in women. It is not the
study of an individual – the stranger remains nameless – but of a
profound psychological need. Plot is sacrificed to the expressionist's concern to reveal another dimension to a repressive society.
Like much expressionist drama, this sketch is pared down to a
monologue designed to release the expressionist scream.

3

Anderson's vision of life in *Winesburg, Ohio* is tied directly to the expressionist form of his stories. The narrator in the introductory sketch tells us simply that there is no such thing as truth, but that there are a great many thoughts, that is, many ways of viewing life, all of which are valid. But human beings, he says, have insisted on experiencing life from just one vantage point, which becomes a position of truth. This distorted view of the world in turn distorts the viewer, who becomes a grotesque, a character "all drawn out of shape." That phrase describes the characters remembered by the old writer in the introduction and subsequently the characters in the stories that follow.

Anderson has made each of his characters memorable by means of a bizarre physical trait or a stylized gesture that isolates the individual from society. Dr. Reefy is not the only character with unusual hands. "Hands" is the title of the first story, the tragedy of an effeminate schoolteacher who tries to reach out to others through touch, but whose motives are misunderstood. The narrator says that the constant movement of Wing Biddlebaum's hands is like "the beating of the wings of an imprisoned bird" (p. 28). In "Respectability," Wash Williams is described as monstrously ugly and dirty like a baboon; even the whites of his eyes look soiled. Yet "he took care of his hands," which are shapely and sensitive (p. 121). Hands dramatize the individual's deep need for connection to others. Even minor characters are sometimes remarkable for their hands. Tom Willy, the saloon keeper, has a flaming birthmark on his hands. When he becomes excited talking to one of his customers, he rubs his hands together, and the red deepens in color "as though the hands had been dipped in blood" (p. 50). Other characters, such as Kate Swift, the teacher, and Elmer Cowley, in "Queer," make their hands into fists and beat at George Willard in a desperate desire to communicate to him some painful truth that they cannot wholly articulate. The Reverend Curtis Hartman puts his fist through the window of the church study. Hands provide a particularly striking aspect of Anderson's expressionist portraits. These hands do not participate in the public handshake or in the caress of lovers, but like the bleeding fist of

Reverend Hartman, they signal the pain and the frustrated desire of these characters to make connections to others.

The eyes of the Winesburg characters are also described in a way that reveals something twisted and obsessive in their nature. The soiled whites of Wash Williams's eyes reflect his vision of the foulness of women. The tiny bloodshot eyes of the baker, Abner Groff, convey the scope of his narrow existence as he seeks revenge on a neighborhood alley cat. In the description of Dr. Parcival's eyes, Anderson uses an elaborate simile to render vividly something alien and closeted in this figure. There was something strange about his eyes, says the narrator: "The lid of the left eye twitched; it fell down and snapped up; it was exactly as though the lid of the eye were a window shade and someone stood inside the doctor's head playing with the cord" (p. 49). Dr. Parcival's refusal of medical assistance when a little girl is thrown from a buggy is like the closing of the window shade. He is left alone with the conviction that someday he will be crucified.

There is a venerable literary tradition of eyes being expressive and central to communication (the poetry of courtly love and Shakespeare's sonnets spring to mind); thus, when a character's eyes are clouded or in any way unusual, interpersonal contact is threatened. On her deathbed, Elizabeth Willard is paralyzed and can no longer speak, but her eyes remain very much alive. She communicates to her son, without the use of words, her desire that he express something for them both: "in her eyes there was an appeal so touching that all who saw it kept the memory of the dying woman in their minds for years" (p. 230). But the eyes of Jesse Bentley that flame with the passionate burning things in his nature are blind with regard to others, and as he grows older his left eyelid develops an uncontrollable twitch. Similarly, his grandson, David Hardy, has "a habit of looking at things and people a long time without appearing to see what he [is] looking at" (p. 75). One of the most alien figures in the book, the albino-like Elmer Cowley, has eyes almost bleached of any color: "his eyes were blue with the colorless blueness of the marbles called 'aggies' that the boys of Winesburg carried in their pockets" (p. 194).

The recurring attention to hands and eyes is part of the expressionist method of repetition. Stein explains her use of repetition as a way of approaching the essence of a character, for she argues that people, carefully observed, are seen to repeat themselves, and in so doing they reveal their essential or ground nature. Anderson focuses on the repetitive behavior of his characters – Dr. Reefy writing down his truths on little pieces of paper, Joe Welling talking excitedly about ideas to casual passersby, Alice Hindman taking her lonely walks. But in his larger vision of a repressed society – "everyone in America really hunger[ing] for a more direct and subtle expression of our common lives than we have ever yet had"[40] – he describes many people living in similar circumstances, enacting the same gestures, so that "the almost universal insanity of society"[41] becomes boldly clear. Even family living patterns are stylized by repetition. Boys and young men in the stories live alone with poor old women (mothers, aunts, grandmothers); they live on the margins of the town. Similarly, young women most often live alone with their fathers, or sometimes their brothers. There are no whole families in the book suggesting complete or fulfilled relationships; Anderson's vision is one of repression, loneliness, and the absence of love. As Walter B. Rideout has observed, the setting is one of the repeated elements in the story. In seventeen of the twenty-two stories, the crisis scene takes place in the evening; some kind of light – a lamp, a fire, some lingering light in the sky – partly relieves the gathering dark. Most of the tales end with the characters going off into total darkness.[42]

But even more striking in *Winesburg, Ohio* is the pattern of people in motion who form something like a procession of the living dead. We know that he thought about the frustrated and defeated characters in his early stories as among the living dead, for he described them in a letter to M. D. Finley, 2 December 1916, as building walls of fear around themselves, inside of which they die.[43] In an earlier letter to Finley he used the image of the procession as part of this vision:

> At times there comes over me a terrible conviction that I am living in a city of the dead. In the office dead voices discuss dead ideas. I go into the street and long rows of dead faces march past. Once I got so excited and terrified that I began to run through the streets. I had a mad impulse to shout, to strike people with my fist. I wanted terribly to awaken them.[44]

This was Anderson's vision of Puritan America. In the introductory sketch, "The Book of the Grotesque," the old writer has a waking dream wherein all the people he has known are being driven in a long procession before his eyes. Afterward he creeps out of bed and writes down what he has seen, describing all the people as grotesques because they live by one truth. These are the characters of Anderson's book, originally titled "The Book of the Grotesque" instead of *Winesburg, Ohio*. The image of the procession is evoked in almost every tale by the central character breaking into a run when he or she reaches a point of insupportable frustration.

Kate Swift, the schoolteacher, is a conventional unmarried woman in the eyes of the townspeople, but, within, her passionate nature yearns for companionship and significant achievement. She takes long walks alone at night; one night she walks for six hours. She half loves her former pupil, George Willard, and in her desire to see his talent as a writer flower, she goes to the newspaper office one night to talk to him. But confused by her love for the boy, she cannot express herself adequately and winds up beating him with her fists, then running out into the darkness. That same night, Reverend Hartman, who for weeks has paced the streets at night imploring God to keep him from his sinful habit of peeping into Kate Swift's bedroom window, bursts into the Winesburg *Eagle* office, shaking a bleeding fist, having broken the window of the church study.

Repeatedly, inarticulate characters in a moment of passion wave their hands in the air and burst into a run. Tom Foster, the shy gentle boy in "Drink," falls in love with the banker's daughter, Helen White. The relationship is socially impossible, and one night Tom goes for a long walk and becomes drunk on a bottle of whiskey. He becomes a grotesque figure moving along the road: "His head seemed to be flying about like a pinwheel and then projecting itself off into space and his arms and legs flopped helplessly about" (p. 218). Jesse Bentley, in "Godliness," who has a vision of being a biblical patriarch, runs through the night begging God to send him a son; years later, when he takes his grandson to sacrifice a lamb, hoping God will finally send a visible sign of his blessing, the scene ends with the flight of the terrified boy from Winesburg. In "Adventure," Alice Hindman, who has been waiting many years for the return of her lover, one night runs out onto the lawn in the rain naked. In the story of the two farmhands, entitled "The Untold Lie," the moment of truth brings Ray Pearson to run across the fields to save his friend, Hal Winters, from marriage. The most vivid scenes in the book are those of characters in grotesque or violent motion: Elizabeth Willard wearing men's clothes and riding a bicycle through the town's main street; Louise Bentley, the estranged daughter of the biblical patriarch, driving her horse and carriage at breakneck speed through the streets of Winesburg; Jesse Bentley's drunken brothers driving along the road shouting at the stars; Hal Winters's father, Windpeter Winters, drunk and driving his team along the railroad tracks directly into the path of an onrushing locomotive. The repetition of such images expresses powerfully the frustration and despair felt by the characters in the small Ohio town. These gestures are another form of the expressionist scream.

4

Considering *Winesburg, Ohio* as an expressionist work further illuminates its historical significance in American literary history. Anderson has long been recognized as an innovator in style, influenced by the vernacular of Mark Twain and responsive to the prose experiments of Gertrude Stein. What Richard Bridgman sees as innovative in Anderson's style is his ability to write in the American vernacular (and its colloquial rhythms) without the use of a child or fool as first-person narrator. Twain used Huckleberry Finn to write in a uniquely American voice; Ring Lardner used Jack Keefe. Anderson, on the other hand, actually established the simple style and its colloquial rhythms as an independent American prose medium.[45] His attempts to forge this unique American voice are seen to flower in the prose style of Ernest Hemingway. But the extent of that influence goes further than Hemingway, and I shall suggest in conclusion that Anderson's expressionist experiments were bolder than Hemingway's and consequently more far-reaching.

In the mainstream of American writing, Anderson's expressionist style represents a sharp break with both realism (including the writing of the naturalists) and impressionism. The latter term is used to describe the psychological realism of Henry James and those he influenced, that is to say, a style of writing that is always suggestive, ambiguous, and heavily dependent on symbolism. The sentences in an impressionist text are characteristically compound-complex, with many qualifying subordinate clauses, and these sentences are often cast in the conditional mode. At the heart of an impressionist novel or story is an experience, emotion, or idea that cannot be explained, only approached obliquely – in what James called a presentiment or what Willa Cather termed "the thing not named." The impressionists (Conrad and Ford were the most eloquent on the subject) acknowledge the relativity of truth, but it is also an aesthetic of evasion, an art of secrets.

Anderson also acknowledged the relativity of truth. At the center of *Winesburg, Ohio* there is despair over the book's central mission – "to express something" for his characters. The view of art in the book undercuts that goal. The artists in *Winesburg, Ohio*, like the old man in the introductory sketch and like Enoch Robinson, are among the least capable of communicating to others, either in their life gestures or in their art. One of the pivotal insights in the book is the realization that comes to Alice Hindman after her adventure on the front lawn: "that many people must live and die alone, even in Winesburg" (p. 120). But Anderson does not retreat with this insight to an art of suggestion, of half-guessed truths. He records instead the struggle to communicate, the effort and the frustration of individuals to explain who they really are. The characters in his fiction are grotesque; yet they are rendered whole in their efforts to express themselves.

"Loneliness," the story of Enoch Robinson, can be viewed as an allegorical statement about art. Robinson is a painter who is remembered in Winesburg as a quiet, dreamy youth. When he was twenty-one he went to New York City, where he attended art school and studied French, hoping some day to finish his art education in Paris. Robinson does not get to France, but it seems likely that the masters with whom he wanted to study there were from the impressionist school. This is reinforced by the description of one of the paintings he shows to a group of artist friends gathered in his room facing Washington Square. Robinson has painted a scene on a country road near Winesburg. In the picture is a clump of elder bushes, inside of which is the body of a woman thrown from a horse. A farmer passing by is shown looking anxiously about in the picture. The woman who has been hurt is at the center of the painting: "She lies quite still, white and still," thinks Robinson, "and the beauty comes out from her and spreads over everything. It is in the sky back there and all around everywhere." But the woman, in fact, is not shown in the picture at all: "I didn't paint the woman, of course. She is too beautiful to be painted" (p. 170). Robinson's painting accords with the aesthetic of the impressionist painter and the literary symbolist, where everything depends on the suggestive power of "the thing not named." But what is significant in the story is that Robinson's painting fails to communicate anything to the audience of friends. They talk of line values and composition, but experience nothing of the emotion that went into the picture. The failure of Robinson's impressionist aesthetic is paralleled in his failure to develop as a man – he remains withdrawn and childlike and retreats into the companionship of imagined people whose presences are threatened every time he comes into contact with real flesh-and-blood people. Robinson's aesthetic fails him, and he becomes "an obscure, jerky little figure, bobbing up and down on the streets of an Ohio town," but Anderson's expressionist art of simplifying, distorting, and exaggerating has rendered Enoch Robinson's character vividly. We learn as much as can be known about this character in a third-person narrative.

Sherwood Anderson argued that good writing has the strong color and form of a Cézanne painting.[46] Hemingway also liked to hold up Cézanne as an artistic model and attributed to the painter important influences on his writing. But in fact, the technical features of the Hemingway style – the choice of language, the structuring of the sentences – have their antecedent in Anderson's prose. What Hemingway learned from Anderson was the power of non-literary words, the four-letter Anglo-Saxon words with their direct appeal to the senses and their hard denotative surfaces. He also learned from Anderson that the arranging of these words in short declarative sentences could have enormous power.

> Dick Boulton looked at the doctor. Dick was a big man. He knew how big a man he was. He liked to get into fights. He was happy. Eddy and Billy Tabeshaw leaned on their canthooks and looked at the doctor. The doctor chewed the beard on his lower lip and looked at Dick Boulton. Then he turned away and walked up the hill to the cottage.[47]

In the structuring of sentences, he learned especially how effective conjunctions were instead of subordinate clauses to convey uninterpreted statements of fact. Subordination creates a hierarchical value structure in a sentence, the main clause being of greatest significance, whereas the use of conjunctions (polysyndeton) gives all the clauses equal value. Implicit in this stylistic choice is the intent to describe and the refusal to judge. This technique is fundamental to Hemingway's clear, hard, nonimpressionistic prose.[48]

Throughout his career Anderson saw himself as an experimental writer. He wrote to Van Wyck Brooks in March 1919, saying that "I want constantly to push out into experimental fields. 'What can be done in prose that has not been done?' I keep asking myself."[49] In his novels in the 1920s, he resisted the formal strictures of plot in favor of looser narrative structures that would include, as he said in the same letter to Brooks, "the purely fanciful side of a man's life, the odds and ends of thought, the little pockets of thoughts and emotions that are so seldom touched."[50] In a letter to Alfred Stieglitz, he described *Dark Laughter* as "a 'fantasy' rather than a novel," with "no realism in it."[51] Hemingway, in order to dispel the anxiety of influence he felt in relation to his literary mentor, wrote *The Torrents of Spring* (1926) to expose what he felt were the thematic weaknesses and stylistic mannerisms of Anderson's fiction. But, ironically, those elements of Anderson's prose he highlighted – the dimension of fantasy, the exaggerated comic-book characters, the loose plot structure, and especially the self-reflexive asides between author and reader – have become valued features of contemporary postmodern fiction. *Winesburg, Ohio* is a classic work of fiction about small-town life in the American Midwest, but as an expressionist work it has a further significance in American literary history in that it provides an important link between the modernism of the first quarter of this century and American writing today.

NOTES

1. *Sherwood Anderson: Selected Letters,* ed. Charles E. Modlin (Knoxville: University of Tennessee Press, 1984), p. 32.
2. *The "Writer's Book" by Sherwood Anderson: A Critical Edition,* ed. Martha Mulroy Curry (Metuchen, N.J.: Scarecrow Press, 1975), p. 85.
3. Quoted by Martha Mulroy Curry in "Anderson's Theories on Writing Fiction," in *Sherwood Anderson: Dimensions of His Literary Art,* ed. David D. Anderson (East Lansing: Michigan State University Press, 1976), p. 94.
4. Kim Townsend, *Sherwood Anderson* (Boston: Houghton Mifflin, 1987), p. 200.
5. Sherwood Anderson, *A Story Teller's Story: A Critical Text,* ed. Ray Lewis White (Cleveland: Case Western Reserve University Press, 1968), p. 272.
6. *Sherwood Anderson's Notebook* (New York: Boni & Liveright, 1926), p. 72.
7. *Letters of Sherwood Anderson,* ed. Howard Mumford Jones and Walter B. Rideout (Boston: Little, Brown, 1953), p. 247.
8. Paul Rosenfeld, *Port of New York: Essays on Fourteen American Moderns* (New York: Harcourt, Brace, 1924), pp. 171–2.
9. *Sherwood Anderson/Gertrude Stein: Correspondence and Personal Essays,* ed. Ray Lewis White (Chapel Hill: University of North Carolina Press, 1972), p. 7.
10. Anderson, *A Story Teller's Story,* pp. 261–3.
11. White, ed., *Anderson/Stein: Correspondence,* p. 82.
12. Ibid., p. 45.
13. Ibid., p. 56.
14. Ulrich Weisstein, ed., *Expressionism as an International Literary Phenomenon* (Paris: Didier, 1973), p. 23.
15. *Letters to Bab: Sherwood Anderson to Marietta D. Finley, 1916–33,* ed. William A. Sutton (Urbana: University of Illinois Press, 1985), p. 85.
16. See Walter B. Rideout, "The Simplicity of *Winesburg, Ohio,*" in *Critical Essays on Sherwood Anderson,* ed. David D. Anderson (Boston: G. K. Hall, 1981), p. 148.
17. See Irving Howe, *Sherwood Anderson* (New York: William Sloane, 1951), p. 99.
18. Ibid.
19. *Sherwood Anderson's Notebook,* pp. 153–4.
20. Anderson, *A Story Teller's Story,* p. 217.

21. Ibid., p. 237.
22. Jones and Rideout, eds., *Letters of Sherwood Anderson*, p. 92.
23. Ibid., p. 93.
24. Sherwood Anderson, *Windy McPherson's Son* (University of Chicago Press, 1965), p. 5.
25. White, ed., *Anderson/Stein: Correspondence*, p. 49.
26. Ibid., p. 68.
27. Ibid., p. 81.
28. Anderson, *A Story Teller's Story*, p. 237.
29. Ibid., p. 263.
30. White, ed., *Anderson/Stein: Correspondence*, p. 17.
31. Ibid., p. 24.
32. Ibid., p. 16.
33. Linda W. Wagner, "Sherwood, Stein, The Sentence, and Grape Sugar and Oranges," in Anderson, ed., *Dimensions of His Literary Art*, p. 82.
34. *Sherwood Anderson's Notebook*, p. 76.
35. *Sherwood Anderson's Memoirs: A Critical Edition*, ed. Ray Lewis White (Chapel Hill: University of North Carolina Press, 1969), p. 348.
36. Anderson, *A Story Teller's Story*, p. 255.
37. White, ed., *Anderson/Stein: Correspondence*, pp. 82–3.
38. Jones and Rideout, eds., *Letters of Sherwood Anderson*, p. 72.
39. Ibid., p. 11.
40. Anderson, *A Story Teller's Story*, p. 234.
41. Jones and Rideout, eds., *Letters of Sherwood Anderson*, p. 44.
42. See Rideout, "The Simplicity of *Winesburg, Ohio*," p. 149. Other repeated images and motifs in the book are discussed by Monika Fludernik in "'The Divine Accident of Life': Metaphoric Structure and Meaning in *Winesburg, Ohio*," *Style* 22 (Spring 1988): 116–35.
43. Sutton, ed., *Letters to Bab*, pp. 17–18.
44. Ibid., p. 15.
45. Richard Bridgman, *The Colloquial Style in America* (Oxford University Press, 1966), p. 153.
46. White, ed., *Anderson/Stein: Correspondence*, p. 83.
47. Ernest Hemingway, *In Our Time* (New York: Scribner, 1958), p. 28.
48. Paul P. Somers, Jr., "The Mark of Sherwood Anderson on Hemingway: A Look at the Texts," *South Atlantic Quarterly* 73 (Autumn 1972): 487–503, suggests that Anderson's influence on Hemingway was chiefly in the use of colloquial language, that matters of syntax were learned from Gertrude Stein. Although it is not possible to determine this question of influence with certainty, it is clear nonetheless

that Anderson demonstrated to Hemingway the usable features of Stein's literary experiments.

49. Jones and Rideout, eds., *Letters of Sherwood Anderson*, p. 46.
50. Ibid.
51. Ibid., p. 129.

3

Winesburg, Ohio and the Autobiographical Moment

MARCIA JACOBSON

IN January 1916, Sherwood Anderson, in a letter to Theodore
Dreiser, lamented, "I have written four long novels and none of
them have been published. I am nearing forty years of age and the
big load of doing a long novel each year also giving eight hours a
day to business is beginning to tell on me. There is a lot of work
ahead I want to do and I want to begin getting publication."[1] He
was in the midst of writing the stories that would eventually make
up *Winesburg, Ohio*, but none had yet been published.[2] Later he
was to claim that in writing "Hands," he knew instantly that he
had taken a dramatic leap forward in his development as a writer.
But in 1916, as he wrote to Dreiser, he felt all the bitterness of a
prolonged apprenticeship in which his literary efforts were not
matched by the affirmation (and, he evidently hoped, the re-
muneration) that publication would have afforded. Given Anderson's practice of incorporating autobiographical material into his
fiction, we might reasonably look to find further expression of his
concern with the gulf between the writer who aspires and writer
who achieves in the project he was working on when he wrote
Dreiser. In writing *Winesburg*, Anderson appraised the size of that
gulf and found himself baffled by it, in the fiction as in his life.

A book whose full title (in the first edition) was *Winesburg, Ohio:
A Group of Tales of Ohio Small-Town Life*, by an author who spent a
substantial part of his youth in Clyde, Ohio, would, of course,
inspire much source-hunting criticism. Despite Anderson's claim
(years after writing the book, in an effort to stress the place of the
imagination in the work of a realistic writer) that almost all of his
characters were based on those living in the Chicago rooming
house in which he wrote *Winesburg*,[3] critics have found numerous
plausible candidates among people whom Anderson knew at vari-

ous periods in his life, in Clyde as well as later in Chicago. Streets and shops in the fictional Winesburg have been shown to have had their origins in real-life Clyde.[4] Anderson himself suggested an autobiographical link in his posthumously published *Memoirs* (1942), again by way of highlighting the transforming powers of the imagination: "I tried to write of my own boyhood but couldn't do it so I invented a figure I called George Willard and about his figure I built a series of stories and sketches called *Winesburg, Ohio*. . . . I firmly believe that anyone reading that book is bound to have a rather sharp impression of my own youth, of what I saw and felt in the people about me."[5] And *Winesburg* itself points to another link, for the voice and outlook of the dedication – "TO THE MEMORY OF MY MOTHER . . . whose keen observations on the life about her first awoke in me the hunger to see beneath the surface of lives" – are clearly those of the narrator.

To cite these connections is not to claim that *Winesburg* is autobiographical in any simple or reductive sense. The presence of youthful and adult perspectives and the division of the author into both protagonist and narrator suggest a complex meditation on autobiographical issues and an exploration of the relationship between past and present selves. At the same time, the fact that we must go outside the fiction itself to find these autobiographical connections should caution us to remember that Anderson chose neither to link himself to his fiction by a literal transcription of his life nor to identify his narrator with George Willard.

In recognizing *Winesburg* as a complex autobiographical fiction, we can also consider it in the context of what Edwin H. Cady calls "the American boy-story," a popular post–Civil War genre that originated with Thomas Bailey Aldrich's *The Story of a Bad Boy* in 1869 and persisted through the second half of the nineteenth century and the early part of the twentieth. Among those boy stories that survive are Mark Twain's *Tom Sawyer* (1876), W. D. Howells's *A Boy's Town* (1890), Hamlin Garland's *Boy Life on the Prairie* (1899), and Booth Tarkington's *Penrod* (1914) – all midwestern stories like Anderson's, and all using fiction to tell the authors' own stories. Cady defines the genre as "distinct from the 'story for boys' . . . in that it contains a depth level at which an imaginative exploration of the nature and predicament of the man-child is carried out."[6] The "predicament," not surprisingly perhaps, typically has reference to a difficult father–son relationship. The author of the boy story explores that relationship, or more often the consequences of that relationship (a more accessible form in which the past persists in the present), in the way he handles the relationship between his narrator (the persona of his adult self) and his protagonist (his child self, remembered and inevitably fictionalized).

Twain, Howells, and Garland provide us with dramatically different examples of the ways in which this might be done. In *Tom Sawyer*, Twain intervenes repeatedly in his story in the role of first-person narrator to undercut Tom's pretensions to grandeur (and when the first-person narrator recedes in the increasingly fictional second half of the book, Huck Finn takes over this role). Though we enjoy Tom's buoyant and irrepressible egotism, Twain seems to have felt a need to exhibit Tom's desire, and by extension his own desire, for affirmation and at the same time his need to punish himself as unworthy. Garland's very different book tells the story of his youthful mastering of one farming skill after another, only to find that his achievements are rapidly made meaningless by the advancement of technology. The adult narrator, however, converts the child's loss into gain as he finds the material of art in the various changes in rural life in the last part of the nineteenth century. Instead of interrupting his story as Twain's narrator does, he distances his story through an intricate structural pattern and through interspersed poems that aestheticize change. Howells splits his younger self in two, "my boy" and "a boy," and in the very active persona of his first-person narrator pushes one or the other to the fore to memorialize (and perhaps exorcise) his morbid and insecure younger self and at the same time, by his more extensive discussion of "a boy," to distract us from "my boy's" difficulties and to imply that his youth as a small-town boy was entirely typical.[7] In contrast to Twain's and Garland's narrators, we can characterize Howells's narrator as manipulative.

What these authors all have in common is their overt identification with their protagonists, if not in the texts, then in the introductory material, and the intimacy they reveal with their protagonists as they tell their stories. Anderson shows his affinity with

them in his splitting himself into the roles of narrator and protagonist as he evokes life in Clyde/Winesburg; he differs from
them in refusing to link narrator and protagonist and in denying
his narrator the intimacy with his protagonist that is appreciably
different from what he feels for his other characters.

To understand the significance of these differences, we might
begin by looking at Anderson's protagonist. As Anderson's own
comment indicates, George is an imaginative transcription of his
younger self – "Jobby" Anderson without his siblings, with
slightly more prosperous parents (who nevertheless bear a distinct
resemblance to his real-life flamboyant and improvident father
and long-suffering, devoted mother), with one job instead of
many, and with a growing ambition to become a writer. In projecting his ambition to write onto young George, Anderson is back-
dating his own development: There is no evidence that the young
Anderson cherished such an ambition – he makes no such claims
in his autobiographies, friends offer no recollections of precocious
literary talent, and there is no body of juvenilia.[8] But in presenting
George as an aspiring artist, Anderson has found a way to dramatize his own still immature hopes for the future and to unify his
book – and he has also found a way to dramatize his continuing
hostility to his father, now seen as the result of uncomfortable
differences in temperament and aspiration rather than as the all-
encompassing hatred that brings his fictional surrogate in his first
novel, *Windy McPherson's Son* (1916), close to murder.

Much of the criticism of *Winesburg* from the 1960s on has
focused on George's development as it is outlined in the course of
the book. Early in *Winesburg*, George's father confronts his son. The
father looks to the boy to be the conspicuous material success in
life he has failed to be, and he is disturbed by his son's dream-
iness, which might jeopardize his chances. "If being a newspaper
man had put the notion of becoming a writer into your mind that's
all right," he concedes, and then adds, "only I guess you'll have to
wake up to do that . . . eh?" (p. 44). But George has his own
notion of what being a writer means, and he boasts fatuously to a
friend that "it's the easiest of all lives to live. . . . Here and there
you go and there is no one to boss you. Though you are in India or
in the South Seas in a boat, you have but to write and there you

are" (p. 134). His former teacher, Kate Swift, recognizes how facile his notion of the artist's life is, and she admonishes him: "You will have to know life. . . . If you are to become a writer . . . you must not become a mere peddler of words. The thing to learn is to know what people are thinking about, not what they say" (p. 163). Her words bring a new soberness and modesty to George as he recognizes that "I have missed something Kate Swift was trying to tell me" (p. 166). With this new maturity, he is ready to leave Winesburg. The book ends with his departure, his father still encouraging him in the only direction the father understands – "Be a sharp one. . . . Keep your eyes on your money. Be awake" (p. 246) – while George himself looks to an uncertain but inviting future, his mind "carried away by his growing passion for dreams" (p. 247). This outline might be fleshed out by consideration of George's encounters with the inhabitants of Winesburg, all of whom, like Kate Swift, sense in George a receptive and responsive spirit, though George does very little to demonstrate this, and by an account of George's fumbling attempts to deal with his attraction to women, which culminates in a few hours of companionship with Helen White in which sex is not quite absent but is deeply submerged.

Two of the best critics who read *Winesburg* in terms of George's development reveal the common assumption that underlies this approach. Edwin Fussell summarizes his view: "*Winesburg* composes as a *Bildungsroman* of a rather familiar type[,] the 'portrait of the artist as a young man' in the period immediately preceding his final discovery of *métier*." Fussell goes on to speak glowingly of George's capacity for learning from all whom he encounters, of learning in particular "to accept the fact of human isolation and to live with it" – a lesson that indicates both his maturity and "his incipient artistic ability."[9] This last phrase makes sense only if we recognize that it is based on Fussell's implicit assumption that George grew up to become the narrator of *Winesburg*, that the book's evocation and celebration of Winesburg's lonely grotesques is the fulfillment of George's discovery. David Stouck, who shares Fussell's notion of the book as a *Bildungsroman* or *Künstlerroman*, is less sanguine about George's achievement, but he is quite explicit about the assumption he shares with Fussell: that George and

Anderson's narrator are one. He argues that although "George has become the sophisticated narrator of *Winesburg, Ohio*," his achievement is finally a failure not of practice but in terms of what we romantically and foolishly hope for from art: "The artist cannot 'save his people'; for only the individual can know himself how it felt to be alive and what life meant. Ironically, in attempting to give dignity and purpose to the lives of his people, the narrator has made them grotesques."[10]

The easy assumption that George and the narrator of *Winesburg* are one is, I believe, not fully justified. Stouck's explanation – "biographical information does not contradict this hypothesis"[11] – is convincing only if we are willing to go outside the text. As I pointed out earlier, Anderson does not make the connection within his text, and it is worth asking why not – or perhaps asking the more answerable question: What is the result of his keeping the narrator and protagonist separate?

We meet Anderson's narrator before we meet George. He figures in the introductory sketch, "The Book of the Grotesque," where he refers to himself as "I" and confides familiarly in us. He tells us of an old writer who has a theory that all people, at least all people he has ever known, become grotesques as they embrace a single ruling idea in life. He also reveals his own character. His stance toward the old man is one of respect. He wants to get at what the man is thinking (he has learned what Kate Swift was trying to teach George), he does not want to laugh at the man's flattering self-image, and, in the end, he learns something from the old man. He is granted a one-time look at the old writer's unpublished "Book of the Grotesque" and thereby learns the old writer's theory about how people become grotesques: It "made an indelible impression on my mind," he tells us. "By remembering it I have been able to understand many people and things that I was never able to understand before" (p. 24).

Much critical ink has been spilled debating the adequacy of the idea of the grotesque as a key to *Winesburg*, a notion given substance by the fact that Anderson at first called his book "The Book of the Grotesque" until his publisher suggested *Winesburg* as a title.[12] This is a particularly tantalizing idea because it makes the old writer another avatar of Anderson himself, this one rather defiantly conceived because he has willfully spurned publication. Regardless of how we understand the old writer, it is worth noting that the narrator does not say that he becomes a convert to the writer's ideas, simply that he learns from them. That is his stance throughout the book: He is not dogmatic, but is interested in what people have to teach him and is eager to do them justice. He is, in fact, a rather likeable character, whereas George is not always so appealing.

We quickly learn that, consistent with the biographical context of the book, the narrator is about a generation older than George. Many of the qualities that distinguish him from George derive from that greater maturity. Whereas George has yet to understand what being a writer really means, the narrator knows the potential of his craft. Although he speaks with the confidence of an established storyteller, he knows that he can do his art only partial justice at this point in his life. When he relates the story of Wing Biddlebaum, "Hands," he observes, "Let us look briefly into the story of the hands. Perhaps our talking of them will arouse the poet who will tell the hidden wonder story of the influence for which the hands were but fluttering pennants of promise" (p. 31). When he tells the story of Louise Bentley in "Godliness," he begins, "Before such women as Louise can be understood and their lives made livable, much will have to be done. Thoughtful books will have to be written" (p. 87). Although the narrator is not ready to write the "hidden wonder story" or one of the "thoughtful books," he makes a start on both by offering us short sketches instead. Sometimes he can only appreciate: He mentions at the beginning of Alice Hindman's story, "Adventure," that her stepfather's story "is an odd one. It will be worth telling some day" (p. 112). But today is not the day for him.

His years give him a historian's perspective. He understands that Winesburg a generation ago (that would be the 1890s) was a world in transition. He remarks at one point that the notion of "a woman's owning herself and giving and taking for her own ends in life" is a "growing modern idea" (p. 115) and thus is not available to Alice Hindman, who pathetically devotes her young life to waiting for the man she loved when she was sixteen. In a contradictory frame of mind, he describes Louise Bentley as "from childhood a neurotic, one of the race of over-sensitive women that in later days industrialism was to bring in such great numbers into the world" (p. 87).

Jesse Bentley's story, "Godliness," goes back two generations and gives the narrator an opportunity to comment on the change that encompasses all of his characters. He begins by addressing us directly – "It will perhaps be somewhat difficult for the men and women of a later day to understand Jesse Bentley" – and then goes on to remind us of all that exists in our world (that of the early twentieth century) that did not exist when this fierce and simple man sought God's intervention in his life:

> The coming of industrialism, attended by all the roar and rattle of affairs, the shrill cries of millions of new voices that have come among us from overseas, the going and coming of trains, the growth of cities, the building of the interurban car lines . . . and now . . . the coming of the automobiles has worked a tremendous change in the lives and in the habits of thought of our people of Mid-America. Books . . . are in every household, magazines circulate by the millions of copies, newspapers are everywhere. . . . Much of the old brutal ignorance that had in it also a kind of beautiful childlike innocence is gone forever. (pp. 70–1)

Most of what happens in *Winesburg* takes place in the midst of this transformation, with George Willard as a reporter contributing to the print explosion that Anderson's narrator notes here.

As the narrator's references to Alice's childhood and Jesse's youth indicate, national history is important to him as it elucidates personal history. His primary passion is personal history; his book is made up of a series of sketches, each illuminating a moment in the life of one or two characters. In telling these stories, we see him again surpassing George. For all of George's centrality to *Winesburg,* he knows very little of what the narrator knows. Most of the characters in *Winesburg* approach George at some point, desperately trying to tell him their stories. They look to him as one who will listen – he is a reporter, after all – and one skilled with words who might be able to translate their inchoate feelings into something that makes sense. But, typically, they are unable to make themselves clear to him. The failure is often theirs, for George is a willing enough listener. But George, too, is often unable to respond. Sometimes he lacks the intuition or the courage to understand: When Wing Biddlebaum approaches him, George thinks, "I'll not ask him about his hands. . . . There's something wrong, but I don't want to know what it is. His hands have something to do with his fear of me and of everyone" (p. 31), a reaction that at once protects both Wing and himself. Sometimes he is too sure of himself: When Elmer Cowley seeks out George to "show him" that he, Cowley, is "like other people" (p. 194), George mistakes Cowley's frustration and aggression for a friendly overture, recalling that "he had long been wanting to make friends with the young merchant and find out what was in his mind. Now he thought he saw a chance and was delighted" (p. 198). But most often George simply does not know enough.

But the narrator knows. A typical *Winesburg* story includes the current events that lead up to the appeal to George as well as the past events that created the current pressure. When Curtis Hartman bursts in on George with the amazing announcement that "God has appeared to me in the person of Kate Swift, the school teacher, kneeling naked on a bed" (p. 155), what can George possibly think? That "the town had gone mad" (p. 165) we will learn in the next story, for the same Kate Swift who had advised him on what it would take to be a writer has just come to him both to indulge and to fight off her desire for him. But the narrator knows of the Reverend Hartman's austere marriage, his lack of faith in himself as a preacher, and the temptation provided by his seeing Kate in her bedroom; he also knows of the monotony of Kate's life and her unfulfilled sexual and emotional needs. As he shares his knowledge with us, he moves freely back and forth between present and past, understanding that the present is a product of the past. Nearly every story in *Winesburg*, in fact, includes a flashback.

The narrator's interest in his characters' pasts and his conviction that the present is to be explained by the past make him not only a historian but also a psychologist.[13] He allows the misogynist Wash Williams to tell his story to George, and in doing so reveals both his own understanding (he, after all, "selects" what he will reveal about Williams) and George's naiveté. George is curious about the ugly, withdrawn man. Because it is common knowledge that Williams hates women, we can assume that George knows this too and in asking Williams if he has ever married expects an ordinary story of betrayal. What Williams reveals instead is the story of a man utterly unable to accept female sexuality. He had come to his marriage a virgin, his virginity preserved "with a kind of religious fervor" (p. 125) (it is not clear that George knows this; this is the narrator's remark to us), and he remembers his wife as a childlike companion who planted a garden with him and as a goddess whom he worshipped: "I kissed her shoes. . . . When the hem of her garment touched my face I trembled" (p. 126). When forced to confront his wife's sexuality through what is admittedly a crude trick, something in him snaps. He emerges a wreck of a man whose story profoundly touches the unsuspecting George. In another instance, the narrator understands, as George cannot, how much Tom Foster's contact with a Cincinnati prostitute before he came to Winesburg has hurt him. No longer able to view women as "quite innocent things, much like his grandmother" (p. 215), but revolted by female sexuality after seeing it in its least romantic form, he tries to ignore his attraction to women. In Winesburg, on the occasion of the story "Drink," he dulls his desire for Helen White, George's girlfriend, with alcohol and babbles semicoherently about making love with her by a seashore, a fairy-tale setting that probably redeems sex from its grossness for this troubled boy. When George reproaches him for talking of Helen, Tom offers an explanation that cannot make sense to George, for he does not know, as we do, thanks to the narrator, that Tom associates sex with degradation: "Helen White made me happy and the night did too. I wanted to suffer, to be hurt somehow. . . . It was like making love" (p. 219).

If we are to believe that George matures to become the narrator of *Winesburg,* we must believe that he has matured a great deal in the years after leaving Winesburg and grant that he has invented a lot of what makes up *Winesburg,* because he could not have absorbed enough to be drawing only on memory. But, of course, people change a great deal in twenty years, and Anderson would never have held that writing is simply a matter of transcribing from life.[14] I do not mean to argue that it is impossible to imagine George having changed enough to have become the narrator of *Winesburg;* Anderson's own life included several dramatic metamorphoses. But there is nothing in *Winesburg* that suggests the process or the mechanism by which such change might happen.

Anderson's interest in psychology helped him to explain what was, but what was to be could be neither predicted nor anticipated.

Years after writing *Winesburg,* Anderson would look back at the two moments that he thought confirmed him as a writer, and he would see mystery in both. In *A Story Teller's Story* (1924), he recalled walking out of his office and out of his incarnation as owner of the Anderson Manufacturing Company: "It came with a rush, the feeling that I must quit buying and selling, the overwhelming feeling of uncleanliness. I was in my whole nature a tale teller. My father had been one and his not knowing had destroyed him. The tale teller cannot bother with buying and selling," he tells us. Buoyed up by that realization, he headed for the door: "Whether at that moment I merely became shrewd and crafty or whether I really became temporarily insane I shall never quite know."[15] Similarly, he insisted, though the manuscript evidence contradicts him somewhat, that "Hands" was written in a trance-like state − the story flowed rapidly and perfectly, not one word was ever changed, and he knew it was good. He tells us at one point in his *Memoirs* that he rose from his desk with "a new gladness," at another that "when it happened in that room, when for the first time I dared whisper to myself, perhaps sobbing, that I had found it, my vocation. I knelt in the darkness and muttered words of gratitude to God," and at another (he does not tire of retelling this story) that he experienced a "sudden almost terrible joy" in which it seemed "that it didn't much matter what happened to me personally during the rest of my life."[16] George, like his creator, will need the equivalent of irresistible grace to make him a writer.

Winesburg not only provides no hint of how George will emerge as a writer, but in fact suggests that the odds are against his doing so. The book includes several failed artists, men who at one time may well have looked as promising to their companions as George does to his. There is the spectacular failure, Enoch Robinson, who left Winesburg for New York when he was slightly older than George. But in the big city, nothing worked. Though he studied art and got to know artists, the narrator explains, "he was always a child and that was a handicap to his worldly development. . . . The child in him kept bumping against things, against actualities like money and sex and opinions" (pp. 167–8). He is literally crippled in a streetcar accident, but like many of Winesburg's inhabitants he is emotionally crippled by his inability to deal with adult sexuality. The narrator describes a picture Enoch paints: a man looking at a grove of trees where a woman who has been thrown from a horse lies suffering. Enoch is tongue-tied and cannot get across to his artistic friends what he would like to explain: "It's a woman and, oh, she is lovely! She is hurt and is suffering but she makes no sound. . . . I didn't try to paint the woman, of course. She is too beautiful to be painted" (p. 170). In his idealizing the woman, he recalls Wash Williams, and his linking of suffering and beauty recalls Tom Foster's linking of suffering and sex. Eventually Enoch marries and becomes a commercial artist – the parallel to Anderson's own life is obvious. Not surprisingly, the marriage is a failure, and business life uncongenial. Enoch finally withdraws into a rented room in which he can live in a world of men and women conjured up by his imagination: "He was like a writer busy among the figures of his brain" (p. 171) – a happy enough life until a second woman intrudes. Wanting her and fearing her at the same time, and now unable to sustain his fantasy life after contact with a real woman who "was so grown up" (p. 176), he is left only with the loneliness that gives his story its title.

Less pathetic, but equally ineffectual as artists, are Winesburg's two doctors – characters who clearly must have had some contact with the larger world when they were young and seem once to have enjoyed some professional success. When we meet them, they are old men, barely sustaining their medical practices, and like nearly everyone in Winesburg trying to figure out how to express themselves. Perhaps it is not fair to think of Doctor Reefy as an artist; still, the narrator tells us that "he was almost a poet in his old age" (p. 221) as he recalls his friendship with Elizabeth Willard, and we might think of the scraps of paper on which he writes his thoughts as minimalist texts, now consigned to his pockets to become hard paper pills that no one reads since his young wife is dead. Doctor Parcival has a better claim to the role of artist. He was once a newspaper reporter like George. He is now a teller of tales, and he has an idea: "You must pay attention to me," he tells George. "If something happens perhaps you will be able to write the book that I may never get written. The idea is very simple. . . . It is this – that everyone in the world is Christ and they are all crucified" (pp. 56–7).

It is even possible to see in George enough affinities to the Winesburg grotesques to imagine that he, too, will become another artist manqué. Like several other citizens, most notably Seth Richmond, he is the son of a passionately devoted mother who is somewhat afraid of the child in whom she sees great possibilities. Although Elizabeth Willard cannot communicate with her son, there is nevertheless "a deep unexpressed bond of sympathy" (p. 40) between them that keeps George in Winesburg and allows him to tolerate his father's criticism until Elizabeth's death. We can imagine a subsequent *Winesburg*-like story in which George's devotion to his mother haunts and hinders him in some way.

We might, for example, anticipate that George would find relationships with women difficult. Anderson offers us the barest of hints. George's adolescent bumbling in his pursuit of women seems unexceptional enough. After having sex with Louise Trunnion, George feels his manhood confirmed – "He had wanted more than anything else to talk to some man" (p. 61) – and at the same time feels like a little boy who has done something wrong, thinking nervously that "she hasn't got anything on me. Nobody knows" (p. 62). Later, he "walks out" with Belle Carpenter, an older woman who is using him to provoke jealousy in the man in whom she is really interested. Although George recognizes her inattention, he sees it as a challenge and does not divine its real reason until Belle's boyfriend rudely awakens him. And finally there is Helen White, the girl for whom George really does care and with whom he shares a moment of closeness at the end of the book – but we shall return to Helen shortly. There is also in George a homoerotic attraction to some of the young men of Winesburg – again, not an exceptional male adolescent experience. There is Seth: "George Willard was older than Seth Richmond, but in the rather odd friendship between the two, it was he who was forever courting and the younger boy who was being courted" (p. 134). And there is Tom Foster, a boy of inexplicable "gentleness" whose

Cincinnati background had brought him into contact with some tough characters; yet "the women in the houses [of prostitution] knew and loved Tom Foster and the tough boys in the gangs loved him also" (p. 212). George, too, is attracted to this boy, angered at first by his talk of Helen, then touched by the vulnerability revealed by his drunkenness: "he felt drawn toward the pale, shaken boy as he had never before been drawn toward anyone" (p. 218). The homoeroticism is, perhaps, a part of the empathy that draws him to such characters as Wash Williams and Enoch Robinson. We can imagine a future in which that capacity to identify with other men would be one of George's gifts as a writer. But recalling George's difficulties with women, in contrast to the ease with which he enters these rather passive homoerotic relationships, we can also imagine a future for him in which he, like a number of other Winesburg characters, would find it impossible to deal with adult female sexuality, and perhaps sexuality in general. Insofar as George, with all of his weaknesses, is an autobiographical surrogate for Anderson, it is to the point that Anderson was delighted by Burton Rascoe's review of the book and thanked him: "Whatever may be the truth about a lot of the fine things you have said concerning *Winesburg,* there is one thing very true and I can't help being glad you said it. Whatever is wrong with the people in the book is wrong with me."[17]

This brings us finally to the last chapters of *Winesburg.* "Death" concludes Elizabeth Willard's story and frees George to leave Winesburg. "Sophistication" and "Departure" are of more interest to me because it is in these two stories that the distance between artistic aspiration and achievement – the gulf voiced in the letter from Anderson to Dreiser quoted earlier, and embodied in George and in Anderson's narrator – becomes most troublesome. *Winesburg* does not end with its narrator enthusiastically celebrating George's achievements and eagerly anticipating his future. This is not a *Bildungsroman* that ends with the protagonist getting the girl and finding a job; it is not a *Künstlerroman* that ends with the young artist triumphantly going forth to "forge in the smithy of [his] soul the uncreated conscience of [his] race."[18] Instead, Anderson hesitates. His uncertainty about his protagonist's future and his recognition that the confident voice of the narrator is a projection of himself that has little basis in life are evident in the murkiness of his style and indeterminacy of the action.

"Sophistication," as its title suggests, marks the apogee of George's growth. In it, he begins to think of himself as an adult, and suddenly the narrator grows pompous and starts speaking for all young men: "There is a time in the life of every boy when he for the first time takes the backward view of life. Perhaps that is the moment when he crosses the line into manhood," he begins, his tentative "perhaps" emphatically overbalanced by the assertiveness with which he continues. Such a boy, he tells us, becomes newly aware of the "limitations of life": "If he be an imaginative boy a door is torn open and . . . he looks out upon the world, seeing, as though they marched in procession before him, the countless figures of men who before his time have come out of nothingness into the world, lived their lives and again disappeared into nothingness" (p. 234). Prior to this, any general comments on human nature had been generated by specific characters in specific situations: Alice Hindman's "Adventure," for example, ends with her "trying to force herself to face bravely the fact that many people must live and die alone, even in Winesburg" (p. 120), after she has spent years closed off from others, waiting for the lover from her girlhood to return. At the end of the book, however, the narrator simply generalizes, and uncharacteristically does so at length: The transient procession of the quoted passage is replaced, as the paragraph continues, first by the image of a wind-blown leaf, then by a wilting stalk of corn. Furthermore, the narrator hides: Instead of forthrightly identifying himself as "I," as he had done earlier, he now presents his ideas as received truths.

And things do not improve. Wanting to be near someone who will understand, George seeks out Helen White, and together they go to the deserted fairgrounds, where they will share an evening of silent understanding and companionship. Again the narrator slips into his pompous mode:

> The place has been filled to overflowing with life. It has itched and squirmed with life and now it is night and the life has all gone away. . . . One conceals oneself standing silently beside the trunk of a tree and what there is of a reflective tendency in his nature is intensified. One shudders at the thought of the meaninglessness of

life while at the same instant, and if the people of the town are his people, one loves life so intensely that tears come into the eyes. (pp. 240–1).

"One"? This is from a narrator who earlier reached out to his readers with an informal and impulsive "you": "It ['The Untold Lie'] is Ray's story. It will, however, be necessary to talk a little of young Hal so that you will get into the spirit of it" (p. 203). Appropriately, this impersonal narrator is literally hidden in the shadows. Luckily we are spared this sort of prose in "Departure," probably because it centers on a very specific event – George boarding the train and leaving Winesburg – that can be handled in a few pages.

We might conclude that the narrator's overblown language reflects his uneasiness as he sets George on the way to adulthood. Not fully convinced that success as a writer will come to George, he now hints that it does not matter, for all life is transient anyway, and all men share in the human tragedy. These seem to be mushy sentiments for an author who has been so precise in particularizing the sufferings of his characters. In fact, these ideas seem rather adolescent. Yet it is clearly the narrator speaking in the quoted passages, not George (as distinct from the narrator) thinking.

It seems that the confident, buoyant narrator of *Winesburg* has regressed at the end of his book to an identification with his protagonist. This, interestingly, makes the book a reversal of what typically happens in an autobiography that recounts childhood or youth. Richard N. Coe, for example, describes the autobiography of childhood as one in which "the formal literary structure is complete at exactly the point at which the immature self of childhood is conscious of its transformation into the mature self of the adult who is the narrator of the earlier experiences."[19] Such a reversal is entirely fitting for an author who was an achieving artist only in the persona of his narrator, but in real life was still an apprentice like his protagonist.

The action of the last two stories further underline Anderson's uncertainty about George and, to the extent that he now identifies himself fully with George, about himself. George's relationship to Helen in "Sophistication" has an adolescent appropriateness to it. He approaches her seeking companionship and understanding only: "He wanted to love and to be loved by her, but he did not want at the moment to be confused by her womanhood" (p. 241), and he gets what he wants. Though they embrace and kiss, they find that their sexuality is in the way of their emotional closeness, and they recoil into "the animalism of youth" (p. 242) as they chase each other home. The story concludes: "they had for a moment taken hold of the thing that makes the mature life of men and women in the modern world possible" (p. 243). It is a troubling conclusion. While we might assent to the notion that understanding makes life in the modern world (defined as "troubled" in this book) possible, we cannot forget, as Anderson seems to be asking us to do here, that that understanding flourishes because sexuality has been set aside. This is hardly a prescription for "mature life."

"Departure" is less troubling, but equally inconclusive. I have spoken of the widely shared assumption that George leaves Winesburg to become a writer. Interestingly, there is no mention of this specific aspiration in the last story, or in the last third of the book, for that matter. We know from "Death" and "Sophistication" that George leaves hoping to find a job on a newspaper. But Anderson, with his career in advertising, knew that everyone who writes is not a writer. Of George's ambition, we are told only that "the young man's mind was carried away by his growing passion for dreams" and that as the town of Winesburg slips past the moving train, it becomes "but a background on which to paint the dreams of his manhood" (p. 247). Not "the dream," but something more vague. So *Winesburg* concludes with the narrator receding into a still adolescent boy who faces an undefined future.

The note of doubt on which *Winesburg* ends contrasts markedly with Anderson's later autobiographical work. Though the process by which he became a writer remains a mystery, the fact of his becoming one takes on an inevitability in his later work. Of course, this is to be explained by the success he finally met, particularly the success of *Winesburg*. But let me conclude by offering another suggestion that is relevant to the substance of *Winesburg* itself. All of Anderson's autobiographical writing – both the autobiographical fiction and the fictionalized autobiographies – concerns itself in some way with the relationship between father and son. Anderson summarized the course of that relationship very simply in his second autobiography, *Tar* (1926): "Hatred of his father came and then, a long time afterwards, understanding."[20] We see that hatred at its most destructive in *Windy McPherson's Son*, where the son nearly murders his father and then spends the rest of his life trying to define himself as something different from his father. And we see the understanding in the autobiographies, where Anderson acknowledges the charm of his father's fantasy-filled life and makes a real effort to understand what it was in his father's time and place that made it impossible for such a man to lead a more responsible life. In these books he also recognizes the extent to which he is his father's son. In his first autobiography, *A Story Teller's Story*, he reflects on his own tendency, even as a child, to "slickness and plausibility," as contrasted with the capacity of one of his brothers for principled action. The difference is to be explained, he says, because "I am the tale teller, the man who sits by the fire waiting for listeners, the man whose life must be led in the world of his fancies. . . . What my father should have been, I am to become."[21] In *Tar* and in *Memoirs* he is equally explicit in picturing himself as realizing his father's gifts as a storyteller.[22]

Winesburg, however, came before Anderson was ready to acknowledge how much he was his father's son: George, like Windy McPherson, albeit less violently, defines himself in opposition to his father. It is probable that Anderson needed success as a writer – needed, that is, to outdo his father as a storyteller – before he could define himself as his father's son. Because that success had not yet come to Anderson, *Winesburg* emerged as a book shaped by his ongoing struggle with his father. It is this conflict that is the source of the relationship between his book and the American boy story in which "the predicament of the man-child" is voiced. Anderson's book, as I noted earlier, differs from other boy stories in its refusal to link narrator and protagonist (until the very end, where the narrator regresses) and in its withholding of intimacy with the protagonist. These differences are really variations within the genre that permit Anderson to approach his "predicament" in his own way. His refusals allow him to dramatize the gulf between aspiration and achievement up to the end, where he deflates his narrator, and they also allow him to present a younger self in the character of George without judgment. We can understand how well Anderson's strategy serves him when we think of Mark Twain as narrator intervening to chastise Tom Sawyer, Hamlin Garland distancing his fictional younger self, or W. D. Howells hiding "my boy." Anderson, still an apprentice as he approached middle age, and still unable to accept himself as his father's son, could not yet evaluate a younger self whose character was shaped by the antagonism and insecurity that resulted from his relationship with his father. What he could do was write a book that embodied that autobiographical moment in which present and past were both very much alive.

NOTES

1. Sherwood Anderson, *Sherwood Anderson: Selected Letters*, ed. Charles E. Modlin (Knoxville: University of Tennessee Press, 1984), p. 4.

2. All information on the writing of *Winesburg* is taken from William L. Phillips, "How Sherwood Anderson wrote *Winesburg, Ohio*," *American Literature* 23 (March 1951): 7–30.

3. Sherwood Anderson, "A Writer's Conception of Realism," in *Sherwood Anderson: The Writer at His Craft*, ed. Jack Salzman, David D. Anderson, and Kichinosuke Ohashi (Mamaroneck, N.Y.: Paul P. Appel, 1979), p. 410.

4. Walter B. Rideout, "The Simplicity of *Winesburg, Ohio*," *Shenandoah* 13 (Spring 1962): 20–1; William A. Sutton, *The Road to Winesburg: A Mosaic of the Imaginative Life of Sherwood Anderson* (Metuchen, N.J.: Scarecrow Press, 1972), p. 440; Kim Townsend, *Sherwood Anderson* (Boston: Houghton Mifflin, 1987), pp. 109–10.

5. Sherwood Anderson, *Sherwood Anderson's Memoirs: A Critical Edition*, ed. Ray Lewis White (Chapel Hill: University of North Carolina Press, 1969), p. 22.

6. Edwin H. Cady, *The Road to Realism: The Early Years, 1837–1885, of William Dean Howells* (Syracuse, N.Y.: Syracuse University Press, 1956), p. 12.

7. For a fuller discussion of these books, see Marcia Jacobson, "The Flood of Remembrance and the Stream of Time: Hamlin Garland's *Boy Life on the Prairie*," *Western American Literature* 17 (November 1982): 227–41, and "William Dean Howells's (Auto)biography: A Reading of *A Boy's Town*," *ALR* 16 (Spring 1983): 92–101.

8. Biographical information is taken from Townsend, *Sherwood Anderson*.

9. Edwin Fussell, *"Winesburg, Ohio:* Art and Isolation," *Modern Fiction Studies* 6 (Summer 1960): 108, 111.

10. David Stouck, *"Winesburg, Ohio* and the Failure of Art," *Twentieth-Century Literature* 15 (October 1969): 151.

11. Ibid., p. 146.

12. Irving Howe's chapter, "The Book of the Grotesque," is a good discussion of *Winesburg* in terms of its grotesques: *Sherwood Anderson* (New York: William Sloane, 1951), pp. 91–109.

13. Frederick J. Hoffman notes Anderson's acquaintance with Freudian ideas, but concludes that his knowledge of psychology was primarily intuitive. *Freudianism and the Literary Mind,* 2nd ed. (Baton Rouge: Louisiana State University Press, 1957), pp. 229–50.

14. The importance of imaginative play for the writer is an idea that surfaces in all of Anderson's autobiographies in justification of his unwillingness or inability to adhere to literal truth. At the beginning of *Tar,* for example, Anderson observes that "the teller of tales, as you must all know, lives in a world of his own. . . . While he is a writer nothing happens but that it is changed by his fancy and his fancy is always at work. Really, you should never trust such a man." *Tar: A Midwest Childhood,* ed. Ray Lewis White (Cleveland: Case Western Reserve University Press, 1969), p. 7. Also see Anderson's "A Writer's Conception of Realism," pp. 401–11.

15. Sherwood Anderson, *A Story Teller's Story: A Critical Text,* ed. Ray Lewis White (Cleveland: Case Western Reserve University Press, 1968), pp. 223, 226.

16. White, ed., *Sherwood Anderson's Memoirs,* pp. 237, 353, 417.

17. Anderson, *Selected Letters,* pp. 11–12.

18. James Joyce, *A Portrait of the Artist as a Young Man* (1916; reprinted New York: Viking Press, 1956), p. 253.

19. Richard N. Coe, *When the Grass Was Taller: Autobiography and the Experience of Childhood* (New Haven: Yale University Press, 1984), p. 9.

20. Anderson, *Tar,* p. 175.

21. Anderson, *A Story Teller's Story,* p. 18.

22. Anderson, *Tar,* p. 100; White, ed., *Sherwood Anderson's Memoirs,* p. 85; also see Anderson, *A Story Teller's Story,* p. 223, passage quoted in this essay.

Motherlove in Two Narratives of Community: *Winesburg, Ohio* and *The Country of the Pointed Firs*

CLARE COLQUITT

1

IN a recent essay, Sandra Zagarell calls attention to an overlooked genre she christens the "narrative of community." This genre comprises works that have often been slighted or misunderstood primarily because they do not partake of Western literature's "preoccupation with the self."[1] Rather, the narrative of community locates its focus in "the collective life of the community" and "seeks to represent what gives the community its identity, what enables it to remain itself":[2]

> Narratives of community ignore linear development or chronological sequence and remain in one geographic place. Rather than being constructed around conflict and progress, as novels usually are, narratives of community are rooted in process. . . . Additionally, writers present details of local life as integral parts of the semiotic systems of the community, and readers are urged to recognize local language and activities like washing and gardening as both absolutely ordinary and as expressions of community history and values. Finally, narratives of community represent the contrast between community life and the modern world directly through participant/observer narrators, and these narrators typically seek to diminish this distance in the process of giving voice to it.[3]

Placing the beginnings of this genre in the early nineteenth century, Zagarell explains that for the predominantly middle-class women who composed narratives of community, the engendering of a genre commemorating communal ties represented "a coherent response to the social, economic, cultural, and demographic changes caused by industrialism, urbanization, and the spread of capitalism."[4] In this volume, Thomas Yingling's interpretation of *Winesburg, Ohio* (1919) as Sherwood Anderson's elegiac re-membering of the death of the collective experience complements Zagarell's analysis of the causes that gave rise to the narrative of community. More specifically, Yingling's understanding of *Winesburg* as "part of a historical moment" in which the small-town ethos of late-nineteenth-century America was effectively destroyed points to a significant psychohistorical parallel linking Anderson to the community of women writers Zagarell describes.

Importantly, Zagarell stresses that despite its origins in nineteenth-century women's culture, the subject of the narrative of community is not gender-bound, nor have women been its only authors. Indeed, Zagarell's study of this evolving genre naturally leads her to Sherwood Anderson when she briefly considers whether or not the "generic center" of *Winesburg* is the narrative of community. Contrasting Anderson's narrative with Charles Dickens's *Little Dorrit*, she argues that "though *Winesburg* is informed by a tension between narrative of community and individual-based narrative, its greater allegiance, thematically and structurally, is to the individualistic tradition of the revolt from the village."[5] Thus, despite its being "specifically structured to accommodate village life," its predominant viewpoint "is the individual-based conviction that everyone has a story to tell; further, George Willard's own story becomes increasingly primary, as he becomes a familiar novelistic character, the sensitive young man from the provinces who leaves to forge his destiny."[6]

Zagarell's analysis of representative American and British narratives of community – Sarah Orne Jewett's *The Country of the Pointed Firs* (1896) and Flora Thompson's *Lark Rise* (1939) – makes it clear that questions of genre and gender are intimately related to the practice of criticism and to the current theoretical debate concerning the shifting shape of the literary canon. Her essay also sheds light on the troubling critical reception of *Winesburg*, a work Carl Bredahl has labeled "a divided narrative."[7] Critics have, in fact, often been divided by their attempts to place Anderson's fiction within traditional generic bounds. Malcolm Cowley, for instance, categorically declares that except for *Winesburg*, Anderson "never even wrote a book": "Those moments at the center of Anderson's often marvelous stories were moments, in general, without a sequel; they existed separately and time-lessly. . . . A book should have a structure and a development, whereas for Anderson there was chiefly the flash of lightning that revealed a life without changing it."[8] Criticizing Anderson's fiction for its nonlinearity, a trait that links *Winesburg* to the narrative of community and, by extension, to a community of women writers, Cowley condescendingly concludes that, structurally, *Winesburg* "lies midway between the novel proper and the mere collection of stories."[9]

In his frustration with Anderson's failure to conform to tradi-tional generic conventions, Cowley implicitly reveals his own pref-erence for the individually centered narrative of the self, more precisely, for the *Bildungsroman*, a novel that typically traces a young man's progress toward adulthood. Not surprisingly, Cowley harshly judges Anderson's semifictional autobiographical works – *A Story Teller's Story* (1924), *Tar: A Midwest Childhood* (1926), and the posthumously published *Sherwood Anderson's Memoirs* (1942) – for being "almost as fictional as the novels." In addition, he laments that the "life" presented in these memoirs provides no "sense of moving ahead in a definite direction."[10] *Winesburg* qualifies as a book only because an "underlying plot or fable, though hard to recognize, is unmistakably present."[11] Cowley maintains that this subtext is Anderson's version of the portrait of the artist as a young man. This view complements Zagarell's in-terpretation, as well as the opinion of many critics who hold that the themes of isolation and communication are central to explicat-ing a work frequently identified as a *Künstlerroman*, a *Bildungsro-man* that focuses on the nascent artist.[12]

Cowley's criticism of Anderson's episodic style echoes the re-marks some critics have made about *The Country of the Pointed Firs*. As Zagarell observes, Jewett's critics have had difficulty in assign-ing *Country* to its appropriate genre; for this reason, "discussion of *Country* has often centered on its status and genre."[13] For instance, Richard Cary's ill-fated attempt to judge *Country* according to "uni-versally accepted [generic] definition[s]" leads him to label Jew-ett's narrative a "paranovel."[14] In a more sensitive assessment of Jewett's fiction, F. O. Matthiessen recognizes that although "for the conventional novel structure [Jewett] had no gift," in the "loosely connected sketches" of *Country* "she has achieved a structure independent of plot."[15]

Despite the similarity of critical responses to *Country* and *Winesburg*, Jewett's and Anderson's books have, to my knowledge, been paired only by Kim Townsend. Yet as Townsend notes in his recent biography, if Anderson was aware of Jewett's narrative, "he never said so."[16] Salient formal and substantive parallels between these works suggest that even if Anderson was not familiar with Jewett's fiction, he drew from the same wellsprings of literary tradition, specifically the narrative of community and the *Künstlerroman*.

As this last statement suggests, I hold that *Country* participates in this latter genre as well. To be sure, the artists portrayed in *Country* and *Winesburg* vary, most importantly in terms of their status as outsider or insider in their respective communities. Age, gender, and professional accomplishments also distinguish the two: The female narrator of *Country* is an older, established writer who hails from the city and journeys to the coast of Maine for a summer holiday, whereas George Willard is a young newspaper reporter with literary aspirations who at the end of *Winesburg* leaves his small hometown behind and sets out for the city "to meet the adventure of life."[17]

Such differences as these, however, only partially account for the conceptual gulf that ultimately separates Anderson's and Jewett's disparate portraits of the artist. In my view, this gulf finds its origins in the Oedipal subtext that operates throughout each work. On a psychological level, both *Country* and *Winesburg* may be seen as narratives about the writer's necessary connection with and separation from powerful maternal figures, that is, about the writer's experience of motherlove.

2

In *A Room of One's Own* (1929), Virginia Woolf addresses this issue in a historical context when she analyzes the plight of women novelists in the early nineteenth century who "had no tradition behind them": "For we think back through our mothers if we are women. It is useless to go to the great men writers for help."[18]

Although directed to women, in some ways this passage aptly defines Anderson's life and art. Townsend's biography, for instance, traces the roots of Anderson's conflicted gender anxiety to his guilt-ridden relationship to his mother: "He would always think of her as Woman, a figure who inspired him to do good, to write. If he could not approach her when she was alive, he would approach her through his works."[19]

My discussion of *Winesburg's* multivalent generic identity reveals another way in which Anderson "thought back through [his] mothers," for to understand that *Winesburg* draws at once from the tradition of the *Künstlerroman* and the narrative of community is to recognize that Anderson was thinking back through his literary forefathers and mothers as well. How conscious Anderson was of his mixed literary ancestry is a matter for speculation. What is certain is that in his public role as the man of letters, Anderson typically felt the need to define his literary heritage as male. Regarding *Winesburg*, however, Anderson was reluctant to acknowledge any sources of literary influence. But as Townsend observes, "the one precedent he did acknowledge and turn to again and again for encouragement in later years was Ivan Turgenev's *Sportsman's Sketches*."[20] Anderson's continual citing of Turgenev may have been a red herring, a half-conscious attempt on the writer's part to steer his readers away from more obvious parallels, that is, from the community of women writers who were also drawn to less conventional narrative forms.

Jewett might well have concurred with Anderson's statements concerning the looseness of form he deliberately sought to achieve in *Winesburg:*

> I have even sometimes thought that the novel form does not fit an American writer, that it is a form which had been brought in. What is wanted is a new looseness; and in *Winesburg* I had made my own form. There were individual tales but all about lives in some way connected. . . . Life is a loose flowing thing. There are no plot stories in life.

For Anderson, *Winesburg* was "something like a novel, a complete story" in which he attempted to convey not the artificial form of a "plot story" but rather "the feeling of the life of a boy growing into young manhood in a town."[21] In the same fashion, Jewett's most famous work is "something like a novel," its completeness deriving from the unifying vision of the unnamed narrator, a skilled storyteller who pieces together the tales she hears and the "characters" she meets into a kind of patchwork quilt of New England sketches that bears witness both to the collective life of Dunnet Landing and to her own artistic powers.

Two early chapters in *Country* allow the reader a behind-the-scenes glimpse of the writer at work. "Mrs. Todd" shows why the narrator, to get any writing done, must ultimately distance herself during the day from the kindhearted gatherer and dispenser of herbs. Mrs. Todd not only provides the narrator with food and lodging but also, as village herbalist, leads her summer guest "on an occasional wisdom-giving stroll."[22] Taking "great advantage" of the narrator's interest in her practice (p. 7), Mrs. Todd initiates her boarder into the healing possibilities of the herbs that grow in her "queer little garden" (p. 3). Soon she depends on the narrator to serve "as business partner during her frequent absences" to gather herbs (p. 6). As if mesmerized by Mrs. Todd, the narrator gladly becomes the herbalist's apprentice, but she quickly discovers that her acceptance of this role precludes any chance to write.

The narrator's dilemma epitomizes the situation that most writers, professional and otherwise, face. Although she joyfully participates in the community life, the "anxious scribe" also recognizes that she must at times remove herself from that life in order to achieve the solitude necessary to write:

> [I]t was not until I felt myself confronted with too great pride and pleasure in the display, one night, of two dollars and twenty-seven cents which I had taken in during the day, that I remembered a long piece of writing, sadly belated now, which I was bound to do. To have been patted kindly on the shoulder and called "darlin'," to have been offered a surprise of early mushrooms for supper, to have had all the glory of making two dollars and twenty-seven cents in a single day, and then to renounce it all and withdraw from these pleasant successes, needed much resolution. Literary employments are so vexed with uncertainties at best, and it was not until the voice of conscience sounded louder in my ears than the sea on the nearest pebble beach that I said unkind words of withdrawal to Mrs. Todd. (pp. 6–7)

The juncture during which the narrator utters her "unkind words of withdrawal" signals an unexpected shift in her developing friendship with Mrs. Todd: "a deeper intimacy seemed to begin" (p. 7). This shift applies as well to the narrator's deepening understanding of the community as a whole. Jewett's narrative suggests that to participate fully in village life, the narrator must extend her knowledge of Dunnet Landing beyond the "pleasant successes" her business enterprise allows.

In "At the Schoolhouse Window," the narrator's choice of an empty classroom for her place of retreat connotes that, however established a writer, she still has something to learn. She also discovers that seclusion does not itself guarantee literary accomplishment. One afternoon the narrator realizes that her writing has yet to capture the "lovely summer cadences" of the life that filters to her through the schoolhouse window (pp. 14–15). Jewett implies that the narrator will never satisfactorily complete "the half-written page" that lies before her until she more wholly "belong[s] to Dunnet Landing" (p. 15). This process involves further schooling in community life. Indeed, the series of initiations the narrator undergoes as her knowledge of Dunnet Landing's inhabitants and rituals grows ultimately enables her to convey in prose the community's "lovely . . . cadences."

Winesburg also depicts the quandaries that confront the writer at work, although at a much earlier stage in a writer's career. In addition, their points of view markedly distinguish Jewett's and Anderson's portraits of the artist, for the third-person narration that Anderson selects to fashion a modernist parable of the alienated artist restricts the reader's insight into the workings of George Willard's mind. Initially the reader's knowledge of George's literary industry derives only from the reports of others, most importantly his mother, who occasionally hovers outside his bedroom door, where she is heartened to hear her son at work: "When she heard the scraping of a chair and the sound of a pen scratching upon paper, she . . . went back . . . to her own room" (p. 45). Elizabeth Willard's attitude of worshipful distance toward her son-as-writer is characteristic of mother/son relations in *Winesburg*. Anderson's description of the distance from which Seth Richmond's mother views her son in "The Thinker" applies to Elizabeth Willard as well: "An almost unhealthy respect for the youth kept the mother for the most part silent in his presence" (p. 130). Just as Mrs. Richmond assumes that her son is a thinker, so Elizabeth Willard, and indeed all the inhabitants of Winesburg, accept on faith George Willard's privileged position as an imminent writer: "The idea that George Willard would some day become a writer had given him a place of distinction in Winesburg" (p. 134). How different the attitude that Mrs. Todd takes toward the narrator of *Country*, when, "partly out of amused curiosity about [her] industries," she one day checks up on "the small scholar" in the schoolhouse (p. 12).

The romantic notion of the godlike artist to which the majority of Winesburg's inhabitants cling sharply delineates Anderson's depiction of the community ethos from that of Jewett. One suspects that the inhabitants of Dunnet Landing would cast a jaundiced eye on the community that worships the artist-to-be rather than honors the word. In fact, *Country* shows that "the habit of reading" has enriched the community of Dunnet Landing and other coastal villages (p. 20). Notably, Captain Littlepage explains that the mighty shipmasters of old particularly revered the word in its myriad manifestations, including the Bible, Shakespeare, and Milton, as well as the "great authorities" on medicine, bee-keeping, and farming. According to the captain, in their studied application to their reading, these shipmasters became "great authorities" themselves: "Most of us old shipmasters came to know 'most everything about something" (p. 21).

With one notable exception, George Willard, Winesburg's inhabitants show little disposition for "the habit of reading." In "Godliness," Harriet Hardy's passionate outburst "I hate books and I hate anyone who likes books" exemplifies in its extremity the general dissatisfaction the community feels toward the printed word (p. 88). Ironically, this frustration exists in spite of the proliferation of books, magazines, and newspapers even in small rural communities like Winesburg. Another passage from "Godliness" points to the source of this paradox: "Books, badly imagined and written though they may be in the hurry of our times, are in every household, magazines circulate by the millions of copies, newspapers are everywhere. In our day a farmer standing by the stove in the store in his village has his mind filled to overflowing with the words of other men" (p. 71). That this account of the debasement of the (printed) word serves as Anderson's parable of the fall is apparent from his subsequent lament: "Much of the old brutal ignorance that had in it also a kind of beautiful childlike innocence is gone forever." Yet when, in this same story, Anderson looks back to the past, to an earlier generation of laborers who had "no desire for words printed upon paper," the reader perceives in the example of Jesse Bentley a profound perversion of "The Word" (p. 71). Indeed, as his last name implies, Bentley's maniacal obsession with his own "godliness" is predicated on his crippling conviction that he himself incarnates The Word.

Bentley's malign mistranslation of The Word reveals that the fall has long since occurred. The corrupting influence of the "peddler[s] of words" in the succeeding (godless) generation has only compounded the sense of loss that Winesburg's inhabitants already feel (p. 163). Unable to find solace in "the habit of reading" or to take comfort in village life, the townspeople are stymied in their efforts to find some means to voice their thoughts and feelings. Small wonder that in her doomed search for "the true word" (p. 224) Elizabeth Willard (like the other grotesques) counts on George to "get something of her passion expressed" (p. 46).

Yet *Winesburg* pointedly reveals that as a writer and a man, George Willard has much to learn. His former schoolteacher, Kate Swift, vainly attempts to instruct the apprentice writer:

> "You will have to know life," she declared, and her voice trembled with earnestness. . . . "If you are to become a writer you'll have to stop fooling with words. . . . It would be better to give up the notion of writing until you are better prepared. Now it's time to be living. . . . You must not become a mere peddler of words. The thing to learn is to know what people are thinking about, not what they say." (p. 163)

To borrow Jewett's term, in many ways George Willard is a "small scholar." Repeatedly *Winesburg* makes it plain that the fledgling writer has not achieved the negative capability necessary for the artist, that he does not understand the meaning of what people say.

No story better illustrates George's immature understanding of art and people than "The Thinker." Unable to write a love story, George dispassionately reaches a decision: "I know what I'm going to do. I'm going to fall in love. I've been sitting here and thinking it over and I'm going to do it" (p. 135). George not only decides to fall in love but also chooses his love object: the beautiful, virginal, and appropriately named Helen White. As he jejunely declares to Seth Richmond, "she is the only girl in town with any 'get-up' to her" (p. 135). Almost against his will, Seth capitulates to George's request to serve as go-between. Although in love with Helen himself, Seth plies George's suit: "He's writing a story, and he wants to be in love. He wants to know how it feels. He wanted me to tell you and see what you said" (p. 139).

"The Thinker" is not the only tale in which Anderson undercuts George's artistic pretensions. "An Awakening" vividly depicts George as "a mere peddler of words." Wandering through town late one night, George finds himself overcome by "the desire to say words": "he said words without meaning, rolling them over on his tongue and saying them because they were brave words, full of meaning. 'Death,' he muttered, 'night, the sea, fear, loveliness' " (p. 185). Immediately following, Anderson illustrates how "oddly detached and apart from all life" George is when, "half drunk with the sense of masculine power" and puffed up by the "brave words" he has just uttered, he is literally brought back to earth by Ed Handby, a man sparing of words (pp. 185, 187). The ease with which George becomes party to Belle Carpenter's plan to provoke her lover's jealousy reveals that George is still no "great authority" on love.

3

Perhaps the most striking difference between *Winesburg* and *Country* lies in the relative importance these authors attach to portraying "the collective life of the community."[23] Although many of Jewett's chapter titles (e.g., "Mrs. Todd," "Captain Littlepage," "William," and "Poor Joanna") clearly indicate that Jewett, like Anderson, believes that "everyone has a story to tell,"[24] Jewett's primary purpose is to justify the outsider narrator's fondness for the maritime community to which she has returned. That her feelings for Dunnet Landing run deep is apparent from her cryptic reaction on catching her first glimpse of the coastal town after an absence of several years: "The process of falling in love at first sight is as final as it is swift in such a case, but the growth of true friendship may be a lifelong affair" (pp. 1–2). In succeeding chapters the narrator focuses on individual characters as well as on large- and small-scale community rituals – family reunions, funerals, neighborhood visits – in a manner that validates her opening remark: "When one really knows a village like this and its surroundings, it is like becoming acquainted with a single person" (p. 1).

Of the rituals depicted, the Bowden family reunion that takes place toward the end of her stay best reveals why the narrator finds this peaceful community "so attaching" (p. 1). Jewett's description of the reunion testifies to the matrilineal organization of this society, emphasizing as it does the community's special reverence for women. Mrs. Todd, for instance, proudly comments that "mother's always the queen," and the narrator observes that though Mrs. Blackett held "court inside the house . . . Mrs. Todd, large, hospitable, and preeminent, was the centre of a rapidly increasing crowd about the lilac bushes" (pp. 98–9). By the time the narrator finds herself partaking of the feast with Mrs. Blackett and Mrs. Todd, that is, with a succession of "large, hospitable, and preeminent" maternal figures, she knows that in spite of her imminent return to the city, she now belongs to the community in ways she did not when she first arrived. Indeed, once she has been warmed by "the primal fires" and "the ancient light" that are released during such rare holidays, the narrator is ready to return to her less peaceful home in the city, for she has reestablished her connections to "the inexhaustible burning heart of the earth," that is, to what Jewett believes is the source of artistic inspiration (p. 96).

In stark contrast to Jewett's Dunnet Landing, Anderson's small midwestern town is devoid of rituals commemorating the essential harmony – and connectedness – of its inhabitants. To be sure, births, marriages, and deaths occur, but the somewhat detached narrator of *Winesburg* only alludes to such happenings and never celebrates them in a manner comparable to the "high days and holidays" Jewett's narrator sympathetically describes (p. 95). Indeed, like the miscarriage that Dr. Reefy's wife suffers in "Paper Pills," rituals in Anderson's narrative also miscarry. Most conspicuous among these aborted rites are Jesse Bentley's successive failures to commemorate his Calvinist conviction that he is one of God's elect. Such aboriginal fires as Anderson presents in "Godliness" and in other tales are invariably snuffed out before the celebrants can warm themselves by "the ancient light" and thereby establish their familial and community ties.

Unlike Dunnet Landing, Winesburg seems not to function as a community; or, perhaps more accurately, the community as such is less Anderson's concern than are the solitary individuals he describes. Numerous critics have observed that Winesburg's inhabitants live in a state of spiritual isolation and anomie. Each of these grotesques might echo Seth Richmond's plaintive avowal that "it's different with me. I don't belong" (p. 137), for none of the central characters in *Winesburg* has a sense of belonging. To paraphrase Zagarell, they may participate in community life, but they do not belong to it.

Cowley labels these grotesques "emotional cripples," but Irving Howe more charitably observes that "the figures of *Winesburg* usually personify to fantastic excess a condition of psychic deformity."[25] Howe is not the only critic who has noticed that *Winesburg* represents a skewed vision of small-town life: "If read as social fiction *Winesburg* is somewhat absurd, for no such town could possibly exist."[26] Indeed, what emerges from Anderson's portrait is a community that lacks coherence, a condition Anderson emphasizes by his seemingly endless gallery of fractured family portraits and splintered marital scenes.

Tellingly, the one community ritual that does bring the inhabitants of Winesburg together, the annual fair, is not of significant narrative interest. Rather, this event principally serves, literally and figuratively, as an opportunity for grandstanding, both on the part of Helen White, who uses the occasion to show off her supposedly sophisticated college professor before the crowds, and on the part of Helen's professor, who calculatingly contemplates the advantages he would accrue should he "marry a woman with money" (p. 236). What details of the fair Anderson provides are set against George Willard's melancholy thoughts as he longs to escape from the fair crowds:

> In the street the people surged up and down like cattle confined in a pen. Buggies and wagons almost filled the narrow thoroughfare. A band played and small boys raced along the sidewalk, diving between the legs of men. Young men with shining red faces walked awkwardly about with girls on their arms. In a room above one of the stores, where a dance was to be held, the fiddlers tuned their instruments. The broken sounds floated down through an open window. . . . The medley of sounds got on young Willard's nerves. Everywhere, on all sides, the sense of crowding, moving life closed in about him. He wanted to run away by himself and think. (p. 237)

This passage illustrates how differently Jewett and Anderson perceive the writer's relationship to community. Rather than "lovely summer cadences," George Willard hears "broken sounds." Whereas the narrator of *Country* is touched to be included in the Bowden family reunion, to be one with the crowd of relatives hovering about the old family homestead like "huge bees . . . swarming in the lilac bushes" (p. 98), George Willard envisions the fair crowds as "cattle confined in a pen."

Importantly, the displacement George feels during the fair is heightened by the sense of loss he feels because his mother has died and by his increasing awareness of the burden she has left him. A threatening sense of entrapment defines his responses to the day's festivities. He needs to distance himself from the young men and women waiting for the dance to start. To regain his sense of identity, he decides "to run away by himself and think." Jewett's narrator undergoes no such crisis when she partakes in one of the key rituals of village life. Indeed, participation in the reunion fosters her sense of self and of the importance of family and community ties. Accordingly, she looks fondly at the high expanse of land that will soon be the site of feasting. In sum, a sense of expansiveness and continuity marks Jewett's celebration of the family reunion and the maternal line; enclosure and fragmentation characterize Anderson's account of the animalistic goings-on of Winesburg's annual fair.

Not surprisingly, George Willard is haunted by what he has felt on the day of the fair. Indeed, as the conclusion of "Sophistication" makes clear, for George and for Helen the fair ultimately "exists" most palpably in the past, not the present. As a result, when George and Helen later return together to the site of the fair, the day's events loom large and evocatively in memory:

> There is something memorable in the experience to be had by going into a fair ground that stands at the edge of a Middle Western town on a night after the annual fair has been held. The sensation is one never to be forgotten. On all sides are ghosts, not of the dead, but of living people. Here, during the day just passed, have come the people pouring in from the town and the country around. . . . The place has been filled to overflowing with life. It has itched and squirmed with life and now it is night and the life has all gone away. The silence is almost terrifying. . . . One shudders at the thought of the meaninglessness of life while at the same instant, and if the people of the town are his people, one loves life so intensely that tears come into the eyes. (pp. 240–1)

This passage exemplifies the axiological gulf that separates Jewett and Anderson. "The thought of the meaninglessness of life" is alien to Jewett. For Anderson, only the artist can impose order and meaning on an essentially meaningless world, one in which both God and mother have died.

4

Given Anderson's darker worldview, the "almost terrifying" silence that brings George and Helen to "the sadness of sophistication" is fitting (p. 234). Throughout *Winesburg*, feelings go unexpressed, and life seems to have "all gone away." What lingers are the ghosts of the living and the dead. Among Winesburg's ghostly inhabitants, the figure who dominates George's life, and indeed the narrative as a whole, is Elizabeth Willard. As Marilyn Judith Atlas points out, Elizabeth Willard's "death hovers over the length of the novel."[27] The narrative suggests, moreover, that George's chief burden as a writer will be to give meaning to his mother's life.

George's relationship with his mother has attracted extensive critical commentary. In analyzing this relationship, critics have observed that Anderson's portrait of Elizabeth Willard is modeled on the writer's memories of his own mother, who, along with his sister Stella, seems to have been the woman who most powerfully marked Anderson's psyche. That Anderson's relationship with his mother was conflicted is poignantly illustrated in his letters and memoirs. One passage from *Sherwood Anderson's Memoirs* is particularly revealing in this regard. Anderson confesses that in the period before he defined himself as a writer, Emma Smith Anderson was, possibly, the only person he had loved: "I do not think I loved anyone, man or woman, with the possible exception of my mother, who had died years before and, perhaps, in a way all such fellows as myself have, I had made a purely romantic figure of her."[28]

One letter composed late in his life shows Anderson painfully "recreat[ing] her figure in [his] own mind."[29] In this letter, which Anderson addressed but never mailed to Paul Rosenfeld, the writer upbraids his close friend for his condescending judgment of the lower class and comments at length on his own feelings for the proletariat. In the process, Anderson attempts to "justify" his role as artist, a defense that causes him to remember the plight of his own working-class mother, who died when Anderson was still a young man:

> You must remember that I saw my own mother sicken and die from overwork. I have myself been through the mill. I have worked month after month in factories, for long hours daily, have known the hopelessness of trying to escape. I have seen my own mother stand all day over a washtub, washing the dirty linen of pretentious middle-class women not fit to tie her shoelaces, this just to get her sons enough food to keep them alive, and I presume I shall never in my life see a working woman without identifying her with my mother.[30]

This letter testifies to the debt Anderson felt toward his mother. Anderson's apologia to Paul Rosenfeld makes plain that Anderson believed that his own success – first as a middle-class businessman and later as a writer – stemmed from the sacrifices his mother endured trying "to get her sons enough food to keep them alive." In Anderson's view, the brevity of his mother's life was thus directly linked to the hardships she faced as the organizing center of her family.[31] Emma Smith Anderson sacrificed herself so that her children might escape life in the mill.

The sense of indebtedness that characterizes George Willard's relationship with his mother undoubtedly finds its principal source in Anderson's anguished memories of his mother: Maternal sacrifice dominates both portraits of "woman." Indeed, whereas suffering and sacrifice define the lives of most women in *Winesburg*, of no character is this more true than Elizabeth Willard, who self-consciously assumes the role of protector in her struggle to see that the "secret something" latent within her son is given the chance to grow (p. 43). Even the chapter titles of the tales centering on Elizabeth Willard, "Mother" and "Death," suggest that Anderson yoked motherhood and death, yet another source for the filial guilt with which his portrait of Elizabeth Willard is steeped.

As with Anderson's description of the fairgrounds, his portrait of George's mother emphasizes her status as one of the ghosts of the living dead; hence the repetition of the term "ghostly" in passages describing Elizabeth or "the disorderly old hotel" that she and her husband failingly maintain (p. 39). Anderson first introduces Elizabeth Willard's spectral figure in "Mother" through her husband's eyes. Tom Willard associates his "tall and gaunt" wife with his failure, for despite his "spruce and business-like appearance," he has succeeded neither personally nor professionally: "The presence of the tall *ghostly* figure, moving slowly through the halls, he took as a reproach to himself. . . . He thought of the old house and the woman who lived there with him as things defeated and done for. The hotel in which he had begun life so hopefully was now a mere *ghost* of what a hotel should be" (p. 39, emphasis added). Lingering about the hallways of the dilapidated hotel, the sickly Elizabeth does in fact seem more ghostly than alive, a haunting figure both to her husband and to her only child.

The ties linking mother and son are importantly connected to George's literary aspirations and to the widening schism between husband and wife. Whereas Elizabeth supports her son's dream of becoming a writer, Tom Willard scorns George's hopes. Tom Willard's sexist yoking of fools, women, and writing sounds especially discordant in the conversation in which he encourages George to direct his energies toward the business world in which the father himself has failed: "You're not a fool and you're not a woman. You're Tom Willard's son and you'll wake up. . . . If being a newspaper man had put the notion of becoming a writer into your mind that's all right. Only I guess you'll have to wake up to do that too, eh?" (p. 44). Tom's criticism of George's youthful dreams is particularly damning, for *Winesburg* makes it clear that in Anderson's lexicon, dreaming is crucial for the artist, the means by which the imagination is warmed by what Jewett calls the "ancient light."

"Mother" reveals another bond between Elizabeth and George: The ghostly Elizabeth is also a woman of dreams. Indeed, mother and son are yoked in a kind of unspoken conspiracy to further George's efforts to write, one "based on a girlhood dream that had long ago died" (p. 40). What that dream entailed is unveiled in a flashback when the narrator describes Elizabeth's unhappy youth and her restless quest to "get something of her passion expressed" (p. 46). Drawn to the touring stage companies that stop in her town, Elizabeth first attempts to realize her dreams by associating herself with these troupes, to which she looks as a means of escape: "She dreamed of joining some company and wandering over the world. . . . Sometimes at night she was quite beside herself with the thought, but when she tried to talk of the matter to the members of the theatrical companies . . . she got nowhere. . . . [T]hey only laughed." Elizabeth's wanderlust later expresses itself in a series of love affairs with traveling salesmen in which "something unexpressed in herself came forth and became a part of an unexpressed something in them." Yet Elizabeth's relationships with these men fail. Although "for a time" Elizabeth feels "released and happy," these short-lived encounters do not further her efforts to express her desires (p. 46). They merely presage the failed communion of her marriage.

Unable to "get something of her passion expressed," Elizabeth transfers her now ghostly dreams to her son. On one of her pilgrimages to her son's room while he is away, she utters an impassioned prayer: "Even though I die, I will in some way keep defeat from you. . . . I ask God now to give me that privilege. . . . I will take any blow that may befall if but this my boy be allowed to express something for us both" (p. 40). Ironically, despite the strength of Elizabeth's desire to protect her son, a desire that reaches its climax when she imagines herself stalking her husband like "a tigress," the word that epitomizes Elizabeth's histrionic imaginings is "unexpressed." Moreover, what Elizabeth does tell her son belies what she believes. The most poignant of the mother/son encounters is the scene in which George tells his mother that he will soon "get out" (p. 47). Playing the devil's advocate, that is, deliberately parodying her husband's words, Elizabeth "wait[s] and tremble[s]" as she challenges George to "wake up": "I suppose you had better wake up. . . . You will go to the city and make money, eh? It will be better for you, you think, to be a business man, to be brisk and smart and alive?" (pp. 47–8). That her words contradict her dreams for George is clear from the narrator's earlier revelation of her closing plea in her prayer: "And do not let him [George] become smart and successful either" (pp. 40–1).

What George understands of his mother's yearnings is never clear. Although "something unexpressed," a "secret bond," undeniably joins mother and son, only the narrator and Anderson's reader comprehend this; George Willard does not. His insight into his mother's character is limited, as his answer to her mock challenge to renounce his artistic dreams suggests: "'I suppose I can't make you understand, but oh, I wish I could,' he said earnestly" (p. 48). The burden George carries with him stems from his half-conscious sense of his mother's unfulfilled desires and his yet-to-be-discovered recognition that the responsibility will ultimately rest on him to find some means to express both her passion and his.

As this summary suggests, Elizabeth's life has been all the more troubling for her relationships with abusive men, primary among them Tom Willard. Recent feminist studies of *Winesburg* show that George follows in his father's footsteps. Nancy Bunge, for instance, notes that throughout most of *Winesburg*, George also routinely exploits women. According to Bunge, in "Sophistication" George comes to a new understanding of male/female relations following his mother's death, when he seeks out Helen White after the fair: "Only companionship can assuage George's new lonely vulnerability; for the first time he wants to talk to a woman, not use her."[32]

George's willingness to use women joins him to the majority of men in Winesburg, from Jesse Bentley and John Hardy in "Godliness," to Enoch Robinson in "Loneliness," to the unnamed fortune hunters in "Paper Pills." In marked contrast to Jewett's *Country, Winesburg* never portrays a loving communion between man and woman. Rather, exploitation dominates all love relations. George's relationships with women typify the emotional distance that only further isolates Winesburg's inhabitants, thereby rendering them increasingly grotesque. From his furtive sexual initiation with Louise Trunnion in "Nobody Knows," to his misinterpretation of Kate Swift's advice in "The Teacher," to his self-serving attempt in "The Thinker" to make Seth Richmond his go-between in a romance with Helen White, George's relationships with women are invariably one-sided. Sexual exploitation, however, is not restricted to men. "An Awakening," for instance, reveals that women are capable of using men sexually as well.

Significantly, Anderson's narrative never devotes a chapter to Helen White. Rather, she is subordinated in the several tales in which she appears, especially in "Sophistication," which links sex, death, and motherhood to George's increasing awareness of his role as man and artist. That George no longer sees Helen as a sexual tool, a vehicle to foster his writing, serves as a sign of his awakening sophistication. Nonetheless, George's chief motive for approaching Helen following his mother's death is self-serving. He believes that she can help him come to terms with his grief: "He wanted someone to understand the feeling that had taken possession of him" (p. 234).

The death of Elizabeth Willard is the turning point in George's life. George's experience of her death, however, bears little resemblance to the emotions Elizabeth herself experiences in the period before she dies. Indeed, what "Death" itself emphatically reveals is the distance between mother and son, for George has no idea that in the last year of her life Elizabeth came close to achieving the passionate release for which she had longed in her relationship with Doctor Reefy. Even before the doctor becomes the object of her love, Elizabeth regularly visits him less for his medical advice than for the chance to voice her thoughts about herself, her marriage, and above all her "passionate longing for adventure" (p. 222). The lonely doctor encourages her visits, which also grant him a means for self-expression: "She and the doctor talked of that [her health] but they talked most of her life, of their two lives and of the ideas that had come to them as they lived their lives in Winesburg" (p. 221).

In the process of listening to Elizabeth's unhappy history, the doctor imagines that she has been transformed into a young and beautiful woman. A similar metamorphosis occurs in one of Anderson's most famous stories, "Death in the Woods," where an old woman's miserable existence is ultimately redeemed by the narrator/artist's power to envision her in death as a beautiful and desirable young woman. Much like the narrator in "Death in the Woods," Doctor Reefy is able to see in "the defeated wife of the Winesburg hotel keeper" the restless young woman she once was. His capacity for reenvisioning Elizabeth's life elevates him to artistic stature. The narrator reports that long after her death, "when he grew older and married a young wife, the doctor often talked to her of the hours spent with the sick woman and expressed a good many things he had been unable to express to Elizabeth. He was almost a poet in his old age and his notion of what happened took a poetic turn" (p. 221). Sadly, this passage indicates that when the doctor and Elizabeth are together, the communication that takes place is partial; in retrospect, the kindly doctor realizes that he was not able to "express a good many things." Their conversations are also apparently more monologue than dialogue: "For the most part the words came from the woman and she said them without looking at the man" (p. 222). In some ways, the doctor similarly fails to look at Elizabeth, for what he ultimately "sees" as he listens to her unhappy life history is "not the tired-out woman of forty-one but a lovely and innocent girl" (pp. 227–8). This positive moment of transformation is accompanied by one of the few occasions in *Winesburg* in which a character genuinely feels love: "Without realizing what was happening," Doctor Reefy "had begun to love her" (p. 226).

For Anderson, if not for Doctor Reefy himself, it is necessary that Elizabeth be "seen" as beautiful, for only then can she deserve love. That Anderson held this to be woman's plight is evident from one of his early letters to Marietta ("Bab") D. Finley, with whom he corresponded for several decades. In October 1916, the period in which he was finishing *Winesburg*, Anderson confessed to Bab, whose love for him was apparently unrequited: "It may seem a terrible pronouncement that woman, although she accept work and make herself a sturdy figure in the world, is yet unworthy of love if she be not physically beautiful and not have that daring fling at life that belongs to the artist but it is true."[33]

In "Mother" and "Death," Anderson reveals that Elizabeth Willard herself had "daring fling[s]" that repeatedly left her unfulfilled. Her situation, though, significantly differs from that of the artist; nothing of permanence results from her adventures. Elizabeth's memory of one episode from her past complements Anderson's "terrible pronouncement" about woman's physical beauty. In "Mother," Anderson conceives of Elizabeth as not desiring to be an artist, but longing to become as beautiful and deserving of love as one former lover thought her to be: "Particularly she remembered one who had for a time been her lover and who in the moment of his passion had cried out to her more than a hundred times, saying the same words madly over and over: 'You dear! You dear! You lovely dear!' The words, she thought, expressed something she would have liked to have achieved in life" (p. 223).

Tellingly, two other characters use these words in the tale describing Elizabeth's death: Doctor Reefy and George Willard. The first such occasion occurs in the doctor's office as Elizabeth is recalling one episode from her past when she desperately beat a horse to make him run faster: "I wanted to go at a terrible speed . . . to get out of town, out of my clothes, out of my marriage, out of my body, out of everything" (p. 227). Moved by her tale, the doctor attempts to console the woman in his arms, "You dear! You lovely dear! Oh you lovely dear!" (p. 227). To borrow Cowley's term, this is "the flash of lightning that reveal[s] a life without changing it."[34] This moment of illumination – and love – is short-lived, for Elizabeth abruptly stops her visits to Doctor Reefy. "The last few months of her life" she spends "hungering for death," a figure Elizabeth personifies as "a strong black-haired youth running over hills" (p. 228).

Elizabeth's conflation of death with the dark bridegroom anticipates the "flash of lightning" that occurs later in "Death" when, as Doctor Reefy had previously done, George Willard sees his mother lying in state and imagines that "someone else lay in the bed before him. . . . The body under the sheets was long and in death looked young and graceful. To the boy, held by some strange fancy, it was unspeakably lovely. The feeling that the body before him was alive, that in another moment a lovely woman would spring out of the bed and confront him, became so overpowering that he could not bear the suspense" (p. 231). The parallel between George's "unspeakably lovely" vision of his mother and the brief moment of communion that Doctor Reefy and Elizabeth Willard enjoyed becomes complete when George leaves this scene saying, "The dear, the dear, oh the lovely dear" (p. 232).

Cowley asserts that "George is released from Winesburg by the death of his mother," while Bunge maintains that Elizabeth's "death finally pushes him out of selfish isolation."[35] One questions the seeming shift in George's character, however, when one reflects that his reaction to his mother's death joins him to the community of men who in *Winesburg* define, exploit, and understand women's desire for expression only in sexual terms. Anderson's "pronouncement" about woman's place within that community seems "terrible" indeed. As Atlas astutely observes, Anderson never allows women a means of escape: "For all the sensitive attention Anderson can pay to his female characters, for all the sympathy he uses to present the story of Louise Bentley, Alice Hindman, and Kate Swift, for all his tenderness toward Elizabeth Willard, he does not, even when the opportunity naturally presents itself, create a female character who wants, and is able, to form her own life."[36] The closing image of Helen White's hurrying – and failing – to meet George's train neatly summarizes Anderson's depiction of women's plight. For women, the train has always just pulled out of the station.

How different George's exit from Winesburg is from "the backward view" that Jewett's narrator enjoys of Dunnet Landing in the concluding chapter of that title. Her summer holiday having reached an end, the narrator feels so closely connected to that community that she half "fear[s]" she will "find [her]self a foreigner" in the home to which she returns (p. 129). Before she boards the ship that will carry her away, she takes one last glimpse at her now empty room: "I and all my belongings had died out of it, and I knew how it would seem when Mrs. Todd came back and found her lodger gone. So we die before our own eyes; so we see some chapters of our lives come to their natural end" (pp. 130–1).

Although the sight of the "empty room" reminds the narrator of the pain Mrs. Todd already feels, the image of the empty nest also connotes that a necessary (re)birth and separation have transpired. Calm acceptance of the cyclical nature of life and, by implication, recognition of the "attaching" nature of communal and mother/daughter ties mark the narrator's bittersweet departure. That her experience of Dunnet Landing is meant to be seen as typical is suggested by her description of one of her last views of the town: "The little town . . . stood high above the flat sea for a few minutes then it sank back into the uniformity of the coast, and became indistinguishable from the other towns" (pp. 132–3).

Where Jewett's *Country* celebrates the universality – and necessity – of thinking back through our mothers, of recognizing even in departure healing community ties, Anderson's *Winesburg* ends with no such backward view commemorating the artist's enlarged understanding of his place within the natural or social order. "Carried away by his growing passion for dreams," George does not even realize the moment when "the town of Winesburg . . . disappear[s]" from view (p. 247). Anderson's ambiguous closing line implies that for George to attain "the backward view of life" (p. 234), he must ultimately do more than conceive of Winesburg as "but a background on which to paint the dreams of his manhood" (p. 247). He must come to terms with those very things he avoids thinking about on the train, "things like his mother's death, his departure from Winesburg, the uncertainty of his future life in the city, the serious and larger aspects of his life" (pp. 246–7). *Winesburg's* dedication to Emma Smith Anderson, who, according to her son, "first awoke in [him] the hunger to see beneath the surface of lives," suggests that George Willard must also find some means to pay tribute to his mother in his art.

NOTES

1. Sandra A. Zagarell, "Narrative of Community: The Identification of a Genre," *Signs* 13 (Spring 1988): 499.
2. Ibid., pp. 503, 520.
3. Ibid., p. 503.

4. Ibid., p. 499.
5. Ibid., p. 513. This term was coined by Carl Van Doren in his influential essay "The Revolt from the Village," *Nation* 12 (October 1921): 407– 12. Van Doren argues that Sherwood Anderson is one of a group of midwestern writers whose characters rebel against the constraints of small-town life. Anderson's own participation in this revolt is still a matter of debate. David D. Anderson, for instance, attacks the position that Anderson rejected the values of community life. See "Sherwood Anderson and the Critics," in *Critical Essays on Sherwood Anderson*, ed. David D. Anderson (Boston: G. K. Hall, 1981), pp. 1–17. In his chapter on Anderson in his fine study *The Revolt from the Village, 1915–1930* (Chapel Hill: University of North Carolina Press, 1969), Anthony Channell Hilfer takes an opposing view.
6. Zagarell, "Narrative of Community," pp. 512–13.
7. A. Carl Bredahl, "'The Young Thing Within': Divided Narrative and Sherwood Anderson's *Winesburg, Ohio*," *Midwest Quarterly* 27 (1986): 422–37. Bredahl broadly defines the term "divided narrative" to describe works that are neither novels nor collections of short stories.
8. Malcolm Cowley, "Introduction," *Winesburg, Ohio* (New York: Viking Press, 1960), p. 11.
9. Ibid., p. 14.
10. Ibid., p. 3.
11. Ibid., p. 14.
12. For representative studies of these themes, see Edwin Fussell, "'Winesburg, Ohio': Art and Isolation," *Modern Fiction Studies* 6 (1960): 106–14, and Glen A. Love, "*Winesburg, Ohio* and the Rhetoric of Silence," *American Literature* 40 (1968): 38–57.
13. Zagarell, "Narrative of Community," p. 521.
14. Richard Cary, *Sarah Orne Jewett* (Boston: Twayne, 1962), p. 131.
15. F. O. Matthiessen, *Sarah Orne Jewett* (Boston: Houghton Mifflin, 1929), p. 101.
16. Kim Townsend, *Sherwood Anderson* (Boston: Houghton Mifflin, 1987), p. 115.
17. *Winesburg, Ohio*, ed. Malcolm Cowley (New York: Viking Press, 1960), p. 246. Other quotations from this standard edition are documented in the text.
18. Virginia Woolf, *A Room of One's Own* (New York: Harcourt, Brace, 1929), p. 79.
19. Townsend, *Sherwood Anderson*, p. 13.
20. Ibid., p. 115.

21. This and the preceding passage are from *Sherwood Anderson's Memoirs,* ed. Paul Rosenfeld (New York: Harcourt, Brace, 1942), p. 289.
22. *The Country of the Pointed Firs,* ed. Marjorie Pryse (New York: Norton, 1981), p. 6. Other quotations are documented in the text.
23. Zagarell, "Narrative of Community," p. 503.
24. Ibid., p. 513.
25. Cowley, "Introduction," p. 15; Irving Howe, *Sherwood Anderson* (New York: William Sloane, 1951), p. 99.
26. Howe, *Sherwood Anderson,* p. 97.
27. Marilyn Judith Atlas, "Sherwood Anderson and the Women of Winesburg," in Anderson, ed., *Critical Essays on Sherwood Anderson,* p. 257.
28. *Sherwood Anderson's Memoirs: A Critical Edition,* ed. Ray Lewis White (Chapel Hill: University of North Carolina Press, 1969), pp. 308–9.
29. Ibid., p. 309.
30. *Letters of Sherwood Anderson,* ed. Howard Mumford Jones and Walter B. Rideout (Boston: Little, Brown, 1953), p. 361.
31. In his memoirs and letters, Anderson repeatedly stated that his mother had died several years earlier than she actually had. In one letter, for instance, Anderson writes that his "mother died when I was about 14"; in fact, Anderson was eighteen. *Sherwood Anderson: Selected Letters,* ed. Charles E. Modlin (Knoxville: University of Tennessee Press, 1984), p. 40.
32. Nancy Bunge, "Women in Sherwood Anderson's Fiction," in Anderson, ed., *Critical Essays on Sherwood Anderson,* p. 245.
33. *Letters to Bab: Sherwood Anderson to Marietta D. Finley, 1916–33,* ed. William A. Sutton (Urbana: University of Illinois Press, 1985), p. 7.
34. Cowley, "Introduction," p. 11.
35. Cowley, "Introduction," p. 14; Bunge, "Women," p. 245.
36. Atlas, "Sherwood Anderson and the Women," p. 264.

5

Winesburg, Ohio and the End of Collective Experience

THOMAS YINGLING

A T the end of "Sophistication," the penultimate story in *Winesburg, Ohio*, the tone of the text takes a positive turn when the reader is informed that George Willard and Helen White have "for a moment taken hold of the thing that makes the mature life of men and women in the modern world possible."[1] We might take this phrase as a means to inquire into the larger vision of the book, for this shift in tone promises a conclusion more positive than what has gone before: Prior to this point, the stories in *Winesburg* have been almost relentless in examining individual lives as narratives of truncated desire. But what this moment in "Sophistication" provides is not simply some bland happy ending. Any optimism registered is markedly undercut by the fact that George and Helen have only temporarily gained access to this mature wisdom and by the implication that it is impossible to say exactly what that key to maturity is. In fact, the narrative is far from blithe about the outcome of maturity. Rather, it encodes access to it as a process of specific, painful loss compensated only by vague promises or intimations of future gain, and it more than strongly hints that George and Helen are allowed this possibility mostly by virtue of "the animalism of youth" (p. 242). Time and again in *Winesburg*, adulthood proves to be a record of how such intimations are lost or betrayed in the course of life's compromises, and the conclusion has hardly enough buoyancy to float the cumulative weight of such histories.

In "Sophistication," the moment of self-knowledge and power (the moment of taking hold of that thing that makes mature life possible) is marked by silence and by play. After having sat quietly touching in the dark of the fairgrounds, George and Helen begin

walking back toward town. They kiss briefly and then are over-
taken by another "impulse":

> In the darkness they played like two splendid young things in a
> young world. Once, running swiftly forward, Helen tripped George
> and he fell. He squirmed and shouted. Shaking with laughter, he
> rolled down the hill. Helen ran after him. For just a moment she
> stopped in the darkness. There is no way of knowing what woman's
> thoughts went through her mind but, when the bottom of the hill
> was reached and she came up to the boy, she took his arm and
> walked beside him in dignified silence. (pp. 242–3)

The language of this passage eases two of the difficulties presented
earlier in the story: George's perception that the world is not
young but old, that he is only one in a procession of "countless
figures of men who before his time have come out of nothingness
into the world, lived their lives and again disappeared into nothingness" (p. 234), and Helen's despair over "the world . . . full of
meaningless people saying words" (p. 239). But if George and
Helen have managed a "meaningful" experience for themselves in
the course of this narrative – if, that is, they have come upon some
"truth," and if it is a truth that is not simply "words" – we as
readers might ask ourselves two further questions. If the key to
meaning lies somewhere other than in words (and this same
premise appears in other stories in *Winesburg*), how could Sherwood Anderson have written a book that had meaning, that was
itself more than just "words"? And what is it about the modern
world that threatens to make the mature life of men and women
impossible in the first place? That is, how has the problem that
threatens the meaningfulness of private relations arisen in material
culture? We shall begin with the second question, taking our cue
from Anderson's language in order to examine those obstacles to
human fulfillment peculiar to "the modern world."

Perhaps the most obvious source of this threat to private meaning is in sexual repression. The text presents frustrated desire as
ubiquitous, the product of an inevitable and universal repression
that causes men and women to misunderstand themselves and
one another. George Willard's mother, for instance, is represented
as in search of "what would be for her the true word" of personal

fulfillment (p. 224), some focus for her "strange wild emotions" that would allow her to articulate "that something unexpressed in herself" (p. 46). But marriage, which she is prompted by others to imagine as "full of some hidden significance" (p. 224), leads only to a barely suppressed murderous rage against her husband. In this, Elizabeth Willard shares the "fate" of frustration that morality visits on the women of Winesburg: Alice Hindman, Kate Swift, and Louise Trunnion, who, like Belle Carpenter, fail to repress their desire and so risk censure. Men also suffer from sexual repression: Wing Biddlebaum, Reverend Hartman, Ray Pearson – the pain and truncated personal experience of each originate in some cultural restriction of his sexuality, fostered, respectively, by homophobia, puritanical religion, and the institution of marriage.

We need not, however, accept this reading of the origins of modern difficulty as the only way to explain it, for such repression may in fact be as much symptom as cause. We might ask what this text so concerned with the price of repression itself represses. We might, that is, move toward a more sustained analysis of the material conditions that frame the meaning of sexuality in the modern world, for despite appearances, that meaning never "naturally" arises from an untroubled cause–effect relation to sexuality. In fact, "sexuality" does not exist apart from the discourses, practices, and institutions that make it meaningful. As such, sexuality is deeply imbricated in the ideological constructions of any given historical moment. The following passages are taken from Antonio Gramsci's comments on "Americanism and Fordism." Gramsci was, like Anderson, the product of a rural culture that had recently (in the 1920s in Italy) fallen under a regime of national industrial regimentation:

> The sexual question [is] increasingly important as a fundamental and autonomous aspect of the economic. . . . The new type of man demanded by the rationalization of production and work cannot be developed until the sexual instinct has been suitably regulated and until it too has been rationalized. . . . This complex of direct and indirect repression and coercion exercised on the masses will undoubtedly produce results and a new form of sexual union will emerge whose fundamental character would apparently have to be monogamy and relative stability.[2]

101

It is true, of course, that repression historically preexisted what Gramsci sees as the rationalization of modern standardized economies and that monogamy also was not a "new" form of social relation in the 1920s. But Gramsci's insights are crucial to clarifying that the social forms and meanings of sexual relations are ideologically, not accidentally or naturally, constructed and that the modern industrial regimes (despite their more overt appearance of encouraging libidinal freedom) have a stake in controlling the social forms through which sexuality is expressed.[3]

To turn the discussion of *Winesburg* toward the question of material history is not to divert it far from its own stated themes. The text displays a consistent (if somewhat incoherent) interest in economic relations, and in trying to piece that interest together we can move across stories and across the narratives of Winesburg individuals in a way that opens for us the whole question whether or not there is any coherent community to Winesburg. Does this book about a town have any collective experience or identity at its center? The question of the collective ought to arise in discussion of *Winesburg*, for although the book examines the burden of separation in some detail, it is itself a collection, a series of stories that cannot but raise the question of what binds it (and the town it represents) together.

We see a number of ritualized moments when the town exists as a single social unit, as in the description of the Winesburg County Fair in "Sophistication": "Farmers with their wives and children and all the people from the hundreds of little frame houses have gathered within these board walls. Young girls have laughed and men with beards talked of the affairs of their lives. The place has been filled to overflowing with life" (p. 240). And we see similar moments in gatherings about the warm winter stove in Ransom Surbeck's poolroom and in the claim that "ideas in regard to social classes had hardly begun to exist" (p. 92), making all citizens of the town "equal." But such moments are awash in nostalgia. The foregoing description of the fairgrounds, for instance, continues: "the life has all gone away. The silence is almost terrifying. . . . One shudders at the thought of the meaninglessness of life while at the same instant, and if the people of the town are his people, one loves life so intensely that tears come into the eyes" (pp. 240–1);

and the moment of masculine bonding and unity in Ransom Surbeck's poolroom comes to a rude end, as we shall discuss later.
Likewise, the claims for an unclassed society are everywhere in the
text proved illusory: The text may claim that "a daughter of a
laborer was in much the same social position as a daughter of a
farmer or a merchant. . . . A girl was 'nice' or she was 'not nice' "
(p. 92), but it is clear that the quality of being nice depends on
sexuality as a function of social class, that Helen White's iconic
significance for the young men of the town, for instance, comes as
much from the privilege of being a banker's daughter as it does
from any virginal appeal.

These nostalgic moments of cultural nondifferentiation are only
the trace of an already vanished harmony and collectivity. As we
now understand it historically, the modern world was witness to
the collapse of collective experience and midwife to the birth of
what John Brenkman calls a "culture of privatization" in Western
societies.[4] Irving Howe perceptively wrote almost forty years ago
that *Winesburg* reads "as if the most sustaining and fruitful human
activities can no longer be performed in public communion but
must be grasped in secret."[5] Its citizens, Howe suggests, "seek not
merely the individual release of a sudden expressive outburst, but
also a relation with each other that may restore them to collective
harmony. They are . . . in search of a ceremony, a social value, a
manner of living, a lost ritual that may, by some means, re-estab-
lish a flow and exchange of emotion."[6] As we continually discover
in *Winesburg*, this loss of collective identity places a terrible burden
on interiority, on how an individual may fashion the meaning of
his or her life.

In writing of the enormous narrative output of the nineteenth
century, Peter Brooks has suggested that "the plotting of the individual or social or institutional life story takes on new urgency
when one no longer can look to a sacred masterplot that organizes
and explains a world,"[7] and the loss of social and institutional
masterplots that accompanies the loss of collective experience in
the modern world places an even greater burden on the individual
life story. Without an exterior world through which to fashion his
or her identity, the modern individual or subject is lost in an urgent
interiority that can only with violence be gathered into coherence.

103

Thus the remarkable quality and quantity of "grotesque" or violent moments in the text. Jacques Lacan, in his reading of Freud's theory of the mirror stage, has suggested that the ideal, coherent self we posit for ourselves in the mirror stage of development (at approximately eighteen months) is a fundamental misrecognition of what remains the contradictory otherness of our bodily and psychic existence; such misrecognition "situates the agency of the ego," Lacan remarks, "in a fictional direction."[8] Lacan's emphasis falls not on cultural recognitions but on familial recognitions, but without the mirroring agency of strong collective structures, identity (considered as self-knowledge anchored in a coherent, stable ego) may be impossible. As institutions falter, so do the identities of those people who have recognized themselves in them. This burden on interiority appears in *Winesburg* in various forms, but virtually all of the adult psychic interiors depicted in the text function according to a theory of character as grotesque. This is outlined for us in the famous preface ("The Book of the Grotesque"), and Doctor Parcival identifies the place of character as that which explains the difficulties in a person's life (who he or she "is") and yet remains curiously twisted and inaccessible to others: "The reason, you see, does not appear on the surface. It lies in fact in my character, which has, if you think about it, many strange turns" (p. 50).

It is this theory of twisted character as originating in an inaccessible but determining interiority that accounts for the utter desolation of so many lives in Winesburg. Despite its notorious interest in sexuality, the more memorable interactions in *Winesburg* come not through bodies touching but in their not touching. Reverend Hartman's voyeuristic interest in Kate Swift and the sexual and emotional loneliness that results from her sublimation of desire in the maternal act of teaching provide a quintessential moment in the text. In the voyeuristic relation, which is our own relation to the people of this text as well, both Kate and Hartman are sealed in a literalized interior that defines and yet isolates them: She is engaged in that act we are engaged in – a private moment of reading. He hypocritically uses religion to ennoble his own private moments of reading. Reverend Hartman would have his words reach and transform Kate Swift, but he does not see the sexual desire that grounds that fantasy: "From wanting to reach the ears of Kate Swift, and through his sermons to delve into her soul, he began to want *also* to look again at the figure lying white and quiet in the bed" (p. 150, emphasis added). Wanting, delving, body, soul, salvation, and sexuality are linked in this passage in a manner beyond the understanding of the one whose psyche links them. The "grotesquerie" here — and what we might call the cruelty of Anderson's vision — lies in the fact that this utter isolation in interiority offers none of the supposed consolations of self-knowledge. Reverend Hartman is as far from self-understanding as one can get. What occurs in the psychic and architectural interiors of Winesburg's inhabitants is truly, as Marcia Jacobson and David Stouck suggest, incommunicable. Kate Swift remains for the town "a confirmed old maid . . . lacking in all . . . human feeling," when in fact "behind a cold exterior the most extraordinary events transpired in her mind" (p. 162). Reverend Hartman's epiphanic shout ("God has appeared to me in the person of Kate Swift, the school teacher, kneeling naked on a bed" [p. 155]) can never signify the psychological process that makes it meaningful. As a statement, it may baffle and amaze, but it will never be intelligible to others.

Similarly, we see Elizabeth Willard kneel outside her son's bedroom, her psychic investment in him hardly less than Reverend Hartman's in Kate Swift. Yet when she, too, comes to what she considers a definitive act of allegiance with her son against his father, she imagines it in terms that could never signify anything except the loss of mental stability:

> No ghostly worn-out figure should confront Tom Willard, but something quite unexpected and startling. Tall and with dusky cheeks and hair that fell in a mass from her shoulders, a figure should come striding down the stairway before the startled loungers in the hotel office. The figure would be silent — it would be swift and terrible. As a tigress whose cub had been threatened would she appear, coming out of the shadows, stealing noiselessly along and holding the long wicked scissors in her hand. (p. 47)

Her transformation into a "figure" in this fantasy is both a reduction and a triumph. It may signify that she no longer has any individuality (her identity and history are erased; she becomes vengeance itself), but it also signifies that she has achieved some ability to signify, to "figure" in the world. (She has never figured for her husband; it is the peculiar burden of her loneliness that he neither sees nor understands her.) And it is wholly in keeping with the crisis of interiority that she imagines this identity for herself through dramatic cliché, for drama is the art form most directly connected to social space and collective participation (being stage-struck allows her to imagine herself in significant social relation to others). As in so many climactic moments in *Winesburg*, however, this desire to act against her husband is never exteriorized. She remains lost in an interiority that the conclusion of the story literalizes: "'I think you had better go out among the boys. You are too much indoors,' she said. 'I thought I would go for a little walk,' replied the son stepping awkwardly out of the room and closing the door" (p. 48).

Rather than read this collapse of collectivity and the concurrent burdens of interiority as "given," or as psychological inevitabilities in the text (and in modern culture), we might ask why they have occurred. Historical materialist analysis would suggest that changes in the social and economic articulations of culture were largely responsible for this modern alienation from public communion. Beginning in the relation to labor and continuing through all forms of social production and exchange, one no longer "knows" any collective dimension in modern industrial culture, but is alienated – first from one's labor and, by extension, from other social relations. Marx's early writings on alienated labor suggest that this alienation from labor is itself twofold. In the object that "confronts [him or her] as an *alien being*" with a reality "*independent* of the producer"[9] and that he or she may not have the economic means to purchase, despite having made it, the worker is alienated by the very product of his or her labor. And in "the *producing activity* itself [the worker] does not affirm himself but denies himself, does not feel well but unhappy, does not freely develop his physical and mental energy but mortifies his body and ruins his mind."[10]

More than half a century after Marx, Gramsci extended this analysis to what he called "the American phenomenon" of "breaking up the old psycho-physical nexus of qualified profes-sional work, which demands a certain active participation of intel-ligence, fantasy and initiative on the part of the worker, and reducing productive operations exclusively to the mechanical, physical aspect."[11] (Gramsci's reference here is to Frederick Winslow Taylor's principles of scientific management and their application to assembly-line production in American factories, what was known as "Fordism.") Only slightly earlier (1914), the American critic Thorstein Veblen wrote that in "modern machine technology the ruling norm is the highly impersonal, not to say brutal, concept of mechanical process, blind and irresponsible," a process, Veblen argued, that debased the human instinct of workmanship.[12]

But the worker's alienation from his or her own productive activity is perhaps less to the point in a discussion of *Winesburg, Ohio* than is the alienation from social relations that occurs in an economy dedicated to commodity production. In a commodity system, according to Marx, exchange value replaces use value in the object (its value is not figured in practical terms but in monetary terms), and this system of market exchange and price erases all other factors in the history of the object. A bushel of wheat no longer appears as the product of concrete labor practices, but as it may be related to other commodities (having the same value as so many shirts, pigeons, and nickels). Thus, as Marx states in *Capital,* "the relations connecting the labour of one individual with that of the rest appear, not as direct social relations between individuals at work, but as . . . social relations between things."[13] It is this loss of the social relation that marks the alienation of modern culture in its most pernicious form (we shall return to this question of labor and commodities later).

Anderson, though not by any means a Marxist, continually expressed his alienation from modern industrial culture: "I could have done without many things, Woolworth Buildings, the Henry Fords, the aeroplane, the automobile, modern Chicago, Detroit, the movies, the radio, Los Angeles, Miami."[14] And like a number of others in his era, he rather blindly imagined black culture in the South as a genuine cultural site not alienated in this way. That he did so mostly in terms consonant with modernist valorizations of "folklife" and the "primitive" (in terms, that is, that were inescapably racist) need not be denied,[15] but part of what Anderson read as genuine in the culture was its resistance to the alienating experience of being a black laborer in the South. That he takes song and dance as figures for that resistance in the passage that follows must be read as the product of a white cultural hegemony that alternately brutalized and infantilized black people, but his intention here seems to have been to celebrate a preindustrial site of cultural collectivity where the body could not be reduced to the sum of its labor:

> A dance in the bodies now. Swaying bodies going empty handed, dancing down a gangplank. . . .
> Dance going down-hill, rest that way, dance then coming up with two hundred pounds on your shoulders.
> Keep dancing, rest dancing.
> De las' sack, de las' sack.
> On Sunday go ride in the white man's engine. Rest riding.
> But keep the song, black man, don't lose the song.
> When you lose that, we've got you, we whites.[16]

Winesburg depicts precious few such moments of self-integration in the field of labor. In fact, Anderson seems elsewhere to acknowledge that such idylls of black life are largely fantastic. But he claimed in an earlier passage in *Notes Out of a Man's Life* that labor was of consuming interest to him, and we might (perhaps) grant him his fantasy of genuine labor in this passage on black stevedores, despite the fact that it is rather uncritically indulged: "When I am not writing all my instincts lead me to go where men are working with their hands. Formerly I also worked with my hands, touched to some purpose wood, iron, brass, brick, stone, the earth. That one should get money by writing, painting, making music is in some way false."[17]

It is difficult to date the historical action of *Winesburg* exactly, but the events of the book seem to take place during the 1890s, the threshold to a century that brought the changes of modern industrial alienation (which had long been effected in Pittsburgh, Cleveland, and Chicago) to even the rural hamlets of the Midwest. As the story "Godliness" would have it, this "most materialistic age in the history of the world" (p. 81) "has worked a tremendous change in the lives and in the habits of thought of our people of Mid-America" (p. 71). Other writers were perhaps more overtly concerned than Anderson to document the effects of alienated labor on the lives and social structures of American culture, but *Winesburg* does not ignore the profound changes taking place in the material, economic structure of American life. In *Poor White*, published one year after *Winesburg*, Anderson lamented that

> a new force that was being born into American life and into life everywhere all over the world was feeding on the old dying individualistic life. . . . Railroads had already been pushed out across the plains; great coal fields from which was to be taken food to warm the blood in the body of the giant were being opened up; iron fields were being discovered; the roar and clatter of the breathing of the terrible new thing, half-hideous, half-beautiful in its possibilities, that was for so long to drown the voices and confuse the thinking of men, was heard not only in the towns but even in lonely farm houses, where its willing servants, the newspapers and magazines, had begun to circulate in ever increasing numbers.[18]

In *Winesburg* we usually see this new force not in its intense and most blatantly alienating form (the urban) but in the forms it takes and the deformations it causes in the lives of a town of "lonely farm houses." Among the most crucial of these effects is the loss of an authentic cultural wisdom and personal integrity identified by Walter Benjamin with storytelling (to which we shall return later): Because of "the millions of copies" of newspapers and magazines, "in our day a farmer standing by the stove in the store in his village has his mind filled to overflowing with the words of other men. . . . The farmer by the stove is brother to the men of the cities, and if you listen you will find him talking as glibly and as senselessly as the best city man" (p. 71). As in "Sophistication," we encounter here the specter of "meaningless people saying words," the notion that language itself is debased in the process of modernization. This debasement occurs not because words have changed but because their use is no longer what defines their value: As with all other commodities, it is only their circulation, their exchange, that "counts."

If *Winesburg* is more often interested in how communication and intention are altered by the modern world's effects on "habits of thought" in this small town, the effects of a materially alienating urban culture still do appear intermittently. For instance, in the story of Tom Foster and his grandmother ("Drink"), we see her as "a half worn-out old woman worker [who] lived with the grandson above a junk shop on a side street. . . . For five years she scrubbed the floors in an office building and then got a place as dish washer in a restaurant. Her hands were all twisted out of shape" (p. 210). Of Tom, we learn that "in Cincinnati he had lived in a neighborhood where gangs of tough boys prowled through the streets. . . . For a while he was messenger for a telegraph company and delivered messages in a neighborhood sprinkled with houses of prostitution" (p. 212). In "Loneliness," we can read Enoch Robinson's crushing alienation from society in New York as partially effected by the urban environment in which it occurs: He "kept bumping against things, against actualities like money and sex and opinions. Once he was hit by a street car and thrown against an iron post. That made him lame" (p. 168). But even when such obvious urban alienation is not the subject of the book, we can see in virtually all of the stories of *Winesburg, Ohio* that labor and its attendant alienations assume a definitive, if elided, role in individual and collective existence. *Winesburg* is populated with people defined as ticket agents, farmers, hotelkeepers, merchants, teachers, doctors, berry-pickers, bankers, carpenters – all of whom are identified by the kind of work they perform and by that work's connection to the "larger" world that lies beyond their small town. This is especially true of those who travel, but even the lowest farmer is dependent on that industrial economy, and not always to his benefit. As David McGranahan has suggested, "before the development of all-weather roads and widespread use of the automobile and truck . . . products were shipped largely by rail, [and] farm incomes suffered from monopolies over transportation links"[19] and from local monopolies in isolated central towns.

Because its location is rural rather than urban, *Winesburg* rings some changes on the typical depiction of modern alienation. Sometimes labor is depicted nostalgically in these stories, as an unalienated activity that seems to ally one with nature. In the following passage, however, note how the stasis and harmony of collectivity are only momentary, dependent, in fact, on the cessation of work:

> It was berry harvest time in Winesburg and upon the station platform men and boys loaded the boxes of red, fragrant berries into two express cars that stood upon the siding. A June moon was in the sky, although in the west a storm threatened, and no street lamps were lighted. In the dim light the figures of the men standing upon the express truck and pitching the boxes in at the doors of the cars were but dimly discernible. Upon the iron railing that protected the station lawn sat other men. Pipes were lighted. Village jokes went back and forth. Away in the distance a train whistled and the men loading the boxes into the cars worked with renewed activity. (p. 136)

Just as often, even this supposedly "preindustrial" labor is a source of alienation, as in "The Untold Lie," where Ray Pearson and Hal Winters discover their commonality (as Ray imagines it) in "a protest against . . . everything that makes life ugly," including the domestic routine of "being a quiet old farm hand" (p. 207). The alienation of labor in "The Untold Lie" is obscured by the issue of masculine social and sexual privilege, but the text pointedly contrasts vitality and routine work: "There they stood in the big empty field with the quiet corn shocks standing in rows behind them and the red and yellow hills in the distance, and from being just two indifferent workmen they had become all alive to each other" (p. 205). In this, *Winesburg* renders problematic a long tradition of cultural fantasy that equates labor on the land with a completely unalienated existence.

But it is in "Queer" that we see the most sustained attention to those new forms of social and economic relation that were reshaping collective life in Mid-America. If we take the early rural economy of "Godliness" as a historical reference point, that economy is motivated mainly by survival and production, but it is a form of labor in which the social relations of workers appear at all events "as their own mutual personal relations, and are not disguised under the shape of social relations between the products of labour."[20] It is not, that is, an economy dominated by commodity relations:

> When Jesse Bentley's father and brothers had come into their ownership of the place, much of the harder part of the work of clearing had been done, but they clung to old traditions and worked like driven animals. They lived as practically all of the farming

111

people of the time lived. . . . The four young men of the family
worked hard all day in the fields, they ate heavily of coarse, greasy
food, and at night slept like tired beasts on beds of straw. (p. 64)

In classic Marxist terms (and not, by contrast, in Stalinist terms),
one would read that obsessive drive toward production as oppressive of all other human instincts and aspirations, including, in
Jesse's case, sensuality and love. Thus, Jesse "wanted to make the
farm produce as no farm in his state had ever produced before and
then he wanted something else. It was the indefinable hunger
within that made his eyes waver," but he "would have given much
to achieve peace and in him was a fear that peace was the thing he
could not achieve" (p. 68).

In family subsistence farming, labor is certainly not unalienated
(one might experience that labor as an externalization of desire
and as labor for another). In "Queer," however, we are faced with
a completely different economic formation, one in which the regime of the commodity has taken hold. No longer producing his
own commodities for exchange in the market (as was the family in
"Godliness"), the merchant of Winesburg enters a relation with
salesmen and customers wherein the commodity itself is of para-
mount importance. In that economy, the social dimensions of the
commodity (both the labor that produced it and/or the use to
which it may be put) are erased. Ebenezer Cowley is not adept in
this role, and so his store sits full of unpurchased goods: "The
honey had stood in the store window for six months. It was for
sale as were also the coat hangers, patent suspender buttons, cans
of roof paint, bottles of rheumatism cure, and a substitute for
coffee that companioned the honey in its patient willingness to
serve the public" (p. 191). The personification in this passage exemplifies what Marx termed the fetishization of the commodity,
and as an advertising writer in Chicago, Anderson surely understood how capitalism exploited this capacity of the product to
appear autonomous, to "speak" to the consumer his own desires
(rather than the producer's or the salesman's desire). It is easy to
read the irony of the commodity's disguise as "servant" when one
understands that the worker is actually the servant of the commodity system (forced to produce and seduced into buying). Certainly it is part of Anderson's rejection of commodity culture that

the object we see peddled in "Queer," the breaking point for young Elmer Cowley in his relation to his father's conspicuous mercantile incompetence, is "a small flat metal substitute for collar buttons" (p. 192) – an object for which need must itself be manufactured, an object at least two removes from immediate usefulness in that it is only a "substitute" for something one can easily do without in the first place. Surely it is only another future "companion" for the inventory of "patient" but unpurchased commodities noted earlier. (Note, too, that honey – an organic substance produced by bees in a process that is the very icon of meaningful, unalienated labor – is reduced to equality with substitute collar buttons in this economy.) It is ironic that Elmer Cowley should imagine his liberation from this system as taking place in service to the very economic mechanism that produces and markets such trifles as substitutes for collar buttons: "He would steal a ride on the local and when he got to Cleveland would lose himself in the crowds there. He would get work in some shop and become friends with the other workmen and would be indistinguishable. Then he could talk and laugh. He would no longer be queer and would make friends. Life would begin to have warmth and meaning for him as it had for others" (pp. 199–200). Because of other moments in *Winesburg* that question the "warmth and meaning" of this life, and because of the tone in which "Queer" concludes, it seems best that we read the desire for collective experience registered in this yearning as wholly misdirected. The outcome of commodity culture, Marx suggested, is precisely this reduction of all labor "to one and the same sort of labour, human labour in the abstract."[21] And if the alienating experience of wage labor can (theoretically) bring one to a new, revolutionary, collective identity, it cannot do so in the relatively uncritical way that Elmer Cowley would accept his role in a process that Veblen described as follows: "The share of the operative workman in the machine industry is (typically) that of an attendant, an assistant, whose duty it is to keep pace with the machine process. . . . His work supplements the machine process, rather than makes use of it. On the contrary the machine process makes use of the workman."[22]

It was in the context of such a breakdown in collectivity and under the regime of these multiple alienations of modernity that

Anderson sought in *Winesburg* to examine the experience of small-town America's entry into a standardized, rationalized modern culture. If collective experience and the social institutions that framed individual existence had indeed collapsed under the pressures of modern alienation, what, other than the accidental or random fact of their geographical commonality, could provide coherence in a collection of narratives set in Winesburg, Ohio, at the precise historical moment of that collapse? Unlike Thomas Hardy, whose vision of modern alienation in England relentlessly cast meaningful social existence in the preindustrial past, Anderson was not quite willing to succumb to the pessimistic vision implied in his rejection of modernity. Neither was he willing simply to dream nostalgically for a more innocent era (when *Winesburg* refers to a historical past, that past is fraught with difficulty and incompleteness). Some fragment, some remainder of vitality escaped the rationalization of modern life for Anderson, and he sought to save two of the great nineteenth-century shibboleths of ·American culture for the twentieth: one, the notion that the commonality of life is grounded in some "universal" experience or quality of human life (i.e., that beneath such negligible differences as class, ethnicity, race, and gender, we are all somehow "the same"); two, the democratic corollary to this, the notion that the individual is powerfully, radically free of material limitation. But even if we grant that it exists, we must also insist that the "universal" is not the same as the "collective."

Given the increasing discourse of sexuality as the origin of the "meaningful" in Western culture at this time,[23] it is not surprising that in its drive to unity, *Winesburg* attempts to anchor some sameness of human existence in sexuality. But the only experience of sexuality common to most of the people of Winesburg is its construction as a private experience completely separate from all other social questions. To say this is not to request public moments of sexuality, but to see, for instance, that women in the text read their sexual oppression as a private "fact" rather than as a political one. And if sexual repression seems the only common link among the citizens of Winesburg, we can see in the story of homosexual panic ("Hands") that even repression is an experience not of sameness but of difference.

114

Eve Kosofsky Sedgwick has used the term "homosexual panic" to identify an internalized ideological condition peculiar to the modern world wherein men undergo a crisis of sexual identity because of the contradiction between the multiple layering of all sexual desire (which is a labile movement between various genders, acts, and fantasies) and the cultural demand for a masculinity defined strictly through regularized heterosexuality. It is in keeping with the logic of patriarchal culture, Sedgwick argues, that the notion of homosexuality be structured as "outside" acceptable male behavior, as a condition that causes panic, denial, and fear if perceived in oneself (or even in others! – so tenuous is the structure of this masculine priority). This is homophobia.

I borrow Sedgwick's term here[24] to suggest that "Hands," most often read as a story about homosexuality, is in fact a story more overtly concerned with homosexual panic and with the privilege of self-assured heterosexual men to mark and brutalize those who differ from them in appearance, speech, and behavior. Indeed, the story of Wing Biddlebaum first overtly concerns homosexuality only when it is intruded into the young man's life as the collective fantasy of townsmen who can imagine no more criminal condition than homosexual desire. Wing (then named Adolph Myers) is as shocked as they at the charges of "a half-witted boy" who becomes "enamored" of the young schoolmaster (p. 32). His conscious intentions are far removed from the reading given his acts by his fellow townsmen, and the fact that Wing does not even read his own touching and poetic intensity in the presence of young men as homoerotically inspired is only further evidence, it seems, of how successfully repressed are these desires. He has no way of understanding the persecution wrought upon him except through an internalized alienation from his own body: "Although he did not understand what had happened he felt that the hands must be to blame" (p. 33). It is difficult to read Anderson's story and realize that seventy years later the specter of homosexual seduction still allows for the persecution of lesbian and gay educators, but our purpose here is to understand that in placing this story as the first in his volume (not counting the prefatory "Book of the Grotesque"), Anderson effectively contravenes any later attempt to construct sexual repression as the core of some universal experience. Repression may be universal (as psychoanalysis suggests), but "Hands" demonstrates quite eloquently how a different material practice frames that repression for all people, especially for those whose sexual minority makes them vulnerable to the disciplinary enforcement of cultural taboos. And if taboos such as those against homosexuality seem, in fact, powerfully collective, we must keep in mind here that what we mean by that term is not simply some expression of a mass ideological imperative. Nazism, for instance, should be read as an exploitation of the desire for collectivity based not on an inclusive and heterogeneous vision of social existence but rather, like the homophobic terror visited on Wing, on a collective vision dependent on the construction (and eradication) of some Other who may act as a scapegoat. When we learn that Wing has taken his pseudonym from "a box of goods seen at a freight station as he hurried through an eastern Ohio town" (p. 33), his abjection and anonymity are ironically answered by a system of exchange that (only slightly less literally) defines and alienates all of its subjects.

The attempt to read sexuality as the origin of identity and (paradoxically) as the private source of common experience fails most spectacularly in the case of homosexuality. Unlike female desire, which supposedly has a number of acceptable social institutions through which it may be expressed (courtship, marriage, motherhood, teaching), homosexual desire may not be articulated in any social or collective form; thus, it may not be expressed at all. More interesting than this attempted circumvention of sexual alienation, perhaps, is *Winesburg's* valorization of heightened interiority as authentic, if only in its psychological theory of character. In the text's gradual focus on the figure of George Willard, however, we can read a more insistent desire to assert that the alienation of the modern does not halt individuals in their quest for a sovereign, "mature" identity: The text would have it that people like George "find themselves" despite social alienation and despite the impossibility of communication.

In one of the text's most interesting stories, "An Awakening," which we might read as George's moment of access to adulthood, his awakening, the development of mature identity is dependent on the ability of some unspecified law to situate the ego beyond its material context in the realm of transcendent power and unity. On an evening ramble that takes him "backstage" in Winesburg, George Willard speaks to himself: "In every little thing there must be order, in the place where men work, in their clothes, in their thoughts. I myself must be orderly. I must learn that law. I must get myself into touch with something orderly and big that swings through the night like a star. In my little way I must begin to learn something, to give and swing and work with life, with the law" (p. 183). This quest for discipline is not sexually innocent, of course; rather, it is strongly linked to the development of adult masculine heterosexuality. The section of the tale directly relating George's experiences on a certain January night begins with a scene of men bragging about their power over women in the poolroom and continues through George's attempt to have sex with Belle Carpenter: "he could achieve in her presence a position he had long been wanting to achieve . . . he thought he had suddenly become too big to be used" (pp. 185–6). This thought makes him "half drunk with the sense of masculine power" (p. 187). Ed Handby, Belle's other suitor (and, it would seem, her genuine lover), intervenes in George's plan, easily casting him aside in their fight; and this is one of George's awakenings in the text. But what takes place between the scene in the poolroom and the walk with Belle Carpenter is a more significant awakening. It is coded to appear as a "universal" moment of self-discovery and as an avenue into collective process and identification.

George leaves the company of others, where his bragging has been induced more by their presence than by his knowledge, it would seem: "The pool room was filled with Winesburg boys and they talked of women. The young reporter got into that vein. . . . As he talked he looked about, eager for attention" (p. 182). Walking in the street, he makes his speech about discipline to himself (quoted earlier), which seems to him "some voice outside of himself" (p. 183) rather than his own (he does not recognize it as the voice of collective masculine fantasy, of male power in patriarchal law). He stands for half an hour in an alleyway, "smelling the strong smell of animals too closely housed and letting his mind play with the strange new thoughts that came to him" (p. 184), and Winesburg fades from immediacy: "he lurked in the darkness, oddly detached and apart from all life" (p. 185). Finally, in a passage with strong Emersonian overtones, he has a moment of visionary understanding that places him in touch with the vast sublimity of the universe and with his own power to mean in it:

> George went into a vacant lot and throwing back his head looked up at the sky. He felt unutterably big and remade by the simple experience through which he had been passing and in a kind of fervor of emotion put up his hands, thrusting them into the darkness above his head and muttering words. The desire to say words overcame him and he said words without meaning, rolling them over on his tongue and saying them because they were brave words, full of meaning. " Death," he muttered, "night, the sea, fear, loveliness." (p. 185)

This moment of authentic "self-knowledge through erasure of self" (the paradox at the center of Emersonian versions of sublimity) occurs not in recognition of his relation to others but in isolation (for Emerson, this occurs in a solitary walk across a bare common),²⁵ and the words George finds to say are curious, at once "without meaning" and "full of meaning." As a mixture of the abstract and the concrete, they place George at the center of an allegory in which everything becomes meaningful through the agency of mental perception. When George's attention returns to the world of Winesburg, he is (for a moment) no longer "oddly detached and apart from all life"; rather, "he felt that all of the people in the little street must be brothers and sisters to him and he wished he had the courage to call them out of their houses and to shake their hands" (p. 185). This sublime moment thus appears to be a key to recognition of the collectivity of social existence.

But even in this moment, George feels a lack: "If there were only a woman here I would take hold of her hand and we would run until we were both tired out. . . . That would make me feel better" (p. 185). It is then that the narrative returns to Belle Carpenter, and during George's walk with her it is suggested that he does not merely wish to run with a woman (as he will with Helen White in "Sophistication") but desires that the woman "surrender herself to him" (p. 187). What we see here is not a simple juxtaposition of male sexual desire to masculine fantasies of transcendental self-awareness or self-awakening, but a recognition of their clear structural sameness. As theorists have recently suggested, both are based on an Oedipal narrative: In the case of the sexual, this should be clear from the overt references to the desire for masculine power and from George's imaging of himself as "big" (i.e., adult) and as connected to law and order. In the case of the transcendental moment, studies by Eric Cheyfitz, Neil Hertz, and Thomas Weiskel[26] all suggest (although with differing emphases) that such moments of sublimity are based in an Oedipal structure wherein a male protagonist is threatened by the overwhelming power, structure, law, and order of some disciplinary Other only to be subsumed into it, only to come to identify with its authority. As Neil Hertz describes it, in the Oedipal moment of the sublime a "disarrayed sequence is converted to one-on-one confrontation," thereby confirming the "unitary [Oedipal] status of the self."[27]

In a script prepared by Emerson in *Nature*, where language provides a masculine power over feminine nature, George's words "death," "night," "sea," "fear," and "loveliness" array an otherwise disarrayed sequence, ordering the supposedly feminine chaos of "nature" that threatens to overwhelm him (in the poolroom, men must brag of their power over women). It is thus appropriate within the logic of Oedipal development that George's path that night follow this trajectory: participating in the discourse of masculine privilege in the company of other men; solitary interiorization of the need for discipline and power; a projection of self-empowerment outward on a generalized female Other (Nature); the need for a figure like Belle Carpenter to confirm this masculine power in the social realm.

As should be painfully clear, this structure of self-discovery or awakening is far from universal; for one thing, it is wholly masculine. Not only are women its primary object of exchange (both imaginatively and literally), but the entire process of Oedipal development has been rejected by feminists as inimical to the psychic life of women. Patricia Yaeger, for one, has called the traditional male sublime "a genre of empowerment based on the simple domination of others" and has examined an alternative "female sublime" that is, to her, "a genre that can include the sociable, the convivial, as well as the grandiose and empowering."[28]

There is not enough space here to do more than briefly indicate the philosophical and psychosexual complexity of this Oedipal matrix in *Winesburg*, but we might also call into question the supposed universality of this sublime moment by reading it as dependent on repression of material differences other than gender. Harold Bloom has suggested that every instance of the sublime, every fresh influx of power in its discourse, is predicated on the repression or forgetting of something anterior to the sublime state (thus its psychological and etymological link to the term "sublimation").[29] In the case of George Willard's cosmic awakening, the forgetting that occasions his sublime moment is a repression of the material signs of economic difference:

> In Winesburg, as in all Ohio towns of twenty years ago, there was a section in which lived day laborers. As the time of factories had not yet come, the laborers worked in the fields or were section hands on the railroads. They worked twelve hours a day and received one dollar for the long day of toil. The houses in which they lived were small cheaply constructed wooden affairs with a garden at the back. The more comfortable among them kept cows and perhaps a pig, housed in a little shed at the rear of the garden. (p. 184)

It is into such a street that George Willard, in quest of the discipline of manhood, wanders, and it is the details of such an existence from which George feels his own alienation:

> The poor little houses lighted by kerosene lamps, the smoke from the chimneys mounting straight up into the clear air, the grunting of pigs, the women clad in cheap calico dresses and washing dishes in the kitchens, the footsteps of men coming out of the houses and going off to the stores and saloons of Main Street, the dogs barking and the children crying – all of these things made him seem, as he lurked in the darkness, oddly detached and apart from all life. (pp. 184–5)

This is part of the story's discourse of masculine sexuality, of course, for this passage distances George from the details of domesticity that accompany adult life in a place like Winesburg: Could he read it rightly, this might be the outcome of George's desire to join a world in which everything has its order. But once again it is important to see that the specific conditions of domesticity are not universal; the specific role of class in their formation is here emphasized – and then forgotten. George later sees this street as "utterly squalid and commonplace" (p. 189), but in the sublime moment concrete details of the social text are forgotten or allegorized. The inclusion of those details in the text, however, suggests that George's power imaginatively to transcend the squalor of life in Winesburg is at least partially determined by an economic privilege he does not recognize.

Repressed in his own thinking, the question of economic difference returns in the story of George's awakening through the figures of Belle Carpenter and Ed Handby. Although she loves him, Belle fears that Ed is not her social equal, and she therefore hides him as her lover and walks occasionally with George merely for the sake of appearance. Ed is defined in terms that set him apart from George: He is almost solely physical, economically poorer, and (because of that) relatively metaphysically impoverished: "The bartender was ready to marry and to begin trying to earn money for the support of his wife, but so simple was his nature that he found it difficult to explain his intentions. His body ached with physical longing and with his body he expressed himself. Taking the milliner in his arms and holding her tightly in spite of her struggles, he kissed her until she became helpless" (p. 181). Unlike George, that is, who has access to words, self-expression, *and money,* the bartender is represented as being limited to mute bodily experiences. And for her part, Belle has no access to power except through her attachment to a man – thus, her subterfuge concerning her lover should be read less as a manipulation of George and more as an index of her own lack of social power. Finally, we must read the access to self-knowledge and masculine power depicted in "An Awakening" as radically limited – not only because it is unavailable to many but also because even for the heterosexual man of relative economic privilege who experiences it, this heightened interiority is no genuine awakening but a fictional moment framing a transitive desire. The structure of individuality, which so strongly grounds action and desire in this text, is based in a misrecognition of the materiality that enables it.

In the figure of George Willard as artist we are offered what is perhaps the most powerful and appealing solution to the problem of modern alienation, and analysis of that figure can return us to the question posed at the beginning of this essay – namely, how it is that a text that expresses doubt about language may nevertheless fashion itself as an authoritative cultural statement. In the widely held reading of George as a surrogate for Sherwood Anderson, and through the myth of the artist's synthetic consciousness, we are offered the paradoxical proposition that *some* isolated individuals (artists, writers especially) may experience and express the will or conscience or experience of the collective not in spite of but by virtue of their isolation. The most famous example of this in modern art is Joyce's conclusion to *A Portrait of the Artist as a Young Man* (1916), where Stephen Dedalus imagines that he will "forge out of the smithy of his soul the uncreated conscience of his race." Like the proposition of the universal sublime analyzed earlier, however, this construction of the artist's solitary access to universal reality is determined within an ideological script it must conceal. Philip Fisher has analyzed the relation between the consolations of this romantic myth of the artist and the world of technological labor in which it took shape:

> The world of rapid creation and rapid replacement, of unskilled repetitive labor, has as its sole exception the artist. . . . No longer working for patrons or commissions, he produces, at his own pace, objects defined by his imagination, fulfilling his own needs alone. . . . Self-employed in a world of larger and larger groupings of employment, he completes each work unaided. . . . As work in general bears fewer and fewer traces of the person of the maker, exactly those forms of art most self-intensive dominate our definition of the work of art.[30]

The artist, that is, becomes a figure through which a culture of alienation may imagine itself less alienated than it really is. But that identification depends on the artist's solitary "vision" and labor.

Perhaps no modern literary critic has more powerfully challenged this notion than Walter Benjamin. In texts such as "The Artist as Producer" and "The Work of Art in the Age of Mechanical Reproduction," Benjamin has given us a highly influential theory of the collective labor of aesthetic practice. In his essay on Nikolai Leskov (translated as "The Storyteller"), Benjamin analyzes how "the art of storytelling is coming to an end"[31] in the alienated, abbreviated world of modern industrial culture. "The art of story-telling," Benjamin writes, "is reaching its end because the epic side of truth, wisdom, is dying out."[32] (As the appeal to "epic" would suggest, Benjamin sees the term "wisdom" here as connected to a collectively oriented art, to an integrated social world.) Storytelling, which has the practical effect of counsel and a collective dimension by virtue of repetition, is being replaced by two lesser forms of modern verbal communication: the novel, written by "the solitary individual who is no longer able to express himself . . . and cannot counsel others,"[33] and information, which reaches its most fragmentary, immediate, but thus collectively useless form in print that "does not survive the moment."[34] Despite its undeniable nostalgia, Benjamin's analysis is not simply a harangue against the avant-garde and a backward-looking desire for traditional cultural forms. What makes his own work "wise" in the epic sense is its insistence that cultural processes be read as part of a social text, that "high culture" (literature, for instance) not be considered an autonomous realm separate from other arenas of social meaning and production. Thus, he relates the wisdom of oral cultures to labors such as spinning and weaving that "go on while they [the stories] are being listened to."[35] For him, such storytelling is a site where "words, soul, eye, and hand are brought into connection,"[36] and the storyteller becomes "the figure in which the righteous man encounters himself."[37] "Righteous" here has the effect not of religious purity but of collective, culturally generated value produced less by fixed belief than through the continual material practice of telling, shaping, listening, and thinking. It is a labor undertaken for all and in which all may participate; it is one's link to cultural value. Without the practice of storytelling, therefore, there would be no "righteous man," because people would have no frame of reference through which to interpret value statements.

In Anderson's work, this same phenomenon comes up again and again, and it is most often linked to the question of industrial standardization and its effects on "a thousand towns of Mid-America."[38] Anderson, having worked in the medium, was particularly aware of how print culture was changing the habits of thought in those towns, disseminating alienation along with information and desire. Until a few years ago, he wrote, each of these towns was "an American village inhabited only by ex-farmers, by artisans, by a few professional men, doctors, lawyers and the like . . . before it became choked with coal dust"[39] ("artisan" is the key word here). In modernized Mid-America, however, as *Winesburg* describes it in a famous passage, a "revolution has in fact taken place," by which "much of the old brutal ignorance that had in it also a kind of beautiful childlike innocence is gone forever" (pp. 70–1). At the end of this passage decrying the spread of automobiles and magazines, the passage begins to wax nostalgic. But the issue for Anderson is not whether or not culture may return to some pristine moment when each individual will be uncontaminated by others; we know from "An Awakening" and "Death" that one is always "urged by some impulse outside himself" (p. 232). As it is for Benjamin, the oral is for Anderson a recognition of the social force of language, be it printed or spoken, and the problem with modern American print culture is that it no longer maintains any link to the social structures in these midwestern towns. It has become only another tool in the hegemony of industrialism. In contrast, "King Coal" offers the reminiscence of sitting on the porch of "an old man who had come [to the town] to rest from his adventures":

> Before us lay the short residence street and at the end of that the main street. The Ford and the movies, products also of the Age of Progress, of the Age of Coal, had not yet come and automobiles of any sort were a rare sight. . . .
>
> For an hour I sat, and it seems to me that in that hour and by way of the old carpet-bagger something came floating down to me from many men of the old times. . . . My lips reformed the sentences the lips of men now dead had formed and, perhaps, caught a little the rhythm, the swing, and the significance of them, and I am sure something of the same sort must have happened to the other lads who had spent the evening with me in the company of the old man. I was at that time intent upon learning the mysteries of the house-painters' trade and as I went through the streets on the next day clad in my overalls I perhaps met one of my companions of the evening before. We stopped and stood talking for a moment.[40]

The linkage among orality, history, and knowledge in this passage participates in the metaphysical yearning for self-presence that Jacques Derrida has suggestively argued is the work of speech as a figure in Western philosophy.[41] But what is more striking is how Anderson links speech to an integrated cultural métier where leisure activity brings one into meaningful contact with others (past and present). The passage even takes up the question of labor-as-trade (now also lost in an "age of coal") as part of this phenomenon.

Thus, George Willard: He is not merely a newspaper reporter, but a confidant, someone to whom others speak. In that, he is the very figure of the storyteller whom Benjamin sees as being lost in the modern world. He both listens and speaks, and always in circumstances that foreground the material context of the narrative. George Willard becomes the focus of collective experience and energy in a moment of transition between an oral culture of proximity that is rapidly disappearing and a print culture (the culture of exchange) rapidly instituting itself as the agent of a "larger" but less authentic culture of industrialism and distance. At least, that is how we are invited to read his status in the text. And yet the collection ends by concentrating on him not as the representative of a collective experience of modern alienation but as a solitary individual for whom the lives of others are only "a background on which to paint the dreams of his manhood" (p. 247). George will be wholly taken up by the modern world of interiority, and in that sense we must read *Winesburg* as an elegy.

NOTES

1. Sherwood Anderson, *Winesburg, Ohio,* ed. Malcolm Cowley (New York: Viking Press, 1960), p. 243. All further references to the text are from this edition and appear in parentheses.

2. Antonio Gramsci, *An Antonio Gramsci Reader: Selected Writings, 1916–1935,* ed. David Forgacs (New York: Schocken Books, 1988), pp. 281–2, 292.

3. See Herbert Marcuse's theory of repressive de-sublimation, in *Eros and Civilization* (Boston: Beacon Press, 1966), and Michel Foucault's reading of power, knowledge, and sexuality in *The History of Sexuality* (New York: Penguin Books, 1978). In a famous assessment in the latter, Foucault writes that "sexuality must not be thought of as a kind of natural given which power tries to hold in check, or as an obscure

domain which knowledge tries gradually to uncover. It is the name given to a historical construct . . . in which the stimulation of bodies, the intensification of pleasures, the incitement to discourse, the formation of special knowledges, the strengthening of controls and resistances, are linked to one another, in accordance with a few major strategies of knowledge and power" (pp. 105–6).

4. John Brenkman, "Mass Media: From Collective Experience to the Culture of Privatization," *Social Text* 1 (Winter 1979): 94–109.

5. Irving Howe, *Sherwood Anderson: A Biographical and Critical Study,* 2nd ed. (Stanford, Calif.: Stanford University Press, 1951), p. 98.

6. Howe, *Sherwood Anderson,* p. 103.

7. Peter Brooks, *Reading for the Plot* (New York: Knopf, 1984), p. xx.

8. Jacques Lacan, *Ecrits: A Selection* (New York: Norton, 1977), p. 2.

9. Karl Marx, "Alienated Labor" (1844), in *The Portable Karl Marx,* ed. Eugene Kamenka (New York: Viking Press, 1983), p. 133.

10. *The Portable Karl Marx,* p. 136.

11. Gramsci, *Selected Writings,* p. 290.

12. Thorstein Veblen, *The Instinct of Workmanship: And the State of the Industrial Arts* (New York: Huebsch, 1914), p. 241.

13. Karl Marx, "Commodities," in *Capital,* Vol. 1, reprinted in *The Portable Karl Marx,* p. 447.

14. Sherwood Anderson, *Notes Out of a Man's Life,* in *Sherwood Anderson's Notebook* (Mamaroneck, N.Y.: Appel, 1970), p. 133.

15. This can be seen not only in the works of white writers but also in the work of African-Americans in the 1920s – in Langston Hughes's tropes of music and dance, for instance. And it is not wholly coincidental that Hughes was supported for some time by an elderly white patron (Mrs. R. O. Mason), whose insistence on the privileging of the primitive was always motivated within a racist ideology. See Arnold Rampersad, *The Life of Langston Hughes* (Oxford University Press, 1986).

16. Anderson, *Notes Out of a Man's Life,* p. 135.

17. Anderson, *Notes Out of a Man's Life,* p. 64.

18. Sherwood Anderson, *The Portable Sherwood Anderson,* ed. Horace Gregory (New York: Viking Press, 1949), pp. 170–1.

19. David McGranahan, "Changes in the Social and Spatial Structure of the Rural Community," in *Technology and Social Change in Rural Areas,* ed. Gene F. Summers (Boulder: Westview Press, 1983), p. 166.

20. *The Portable Karl Marx,* p. 453.

21. *The Portable Karl Marx,* p. 441.

22. Veblen, *The Instinct of Workmanship,* pp. 306–7.

23. See Foucault, *The History of Sexuality,* John D'Emilio and Estelle B. Freedman, *Intimate Matters: A History of Sexuality in America* (New York: Harper & Row, 1988), and Frederic Jameson's comment in *The Political Unconscious* (Ithaca, N.Y.: Cornell University Press, 1981) that if "the preliminary isolation of sexual experience . . . enables its constitutive features to carry a wider symbolic meaning . . . its symbolic possibilities are dependent on its preliminary exclusion from the social field" (p. 64).

24. The notion of homosexual panic is preliminarily developed in Eve Kosofsky Sedgwick, *Between Men: English Literature and Male Homosocial Desire* (New York: Columbia University Press, 1985), and more thoroughly in her more recent work, especially "The Beast in the Closet: James and the Writing of Homosexual Panic," in *Sex, Politics, and Science in the Nineteenth-Century Novel,* ed. Ruth Bernard Yeazell (Baltimore: Johns Hopkins University Press, 1986).

25. The apposite passage from *Nature* (1836): "Standing on the bare ground, – my head bathed by the blithe air and uplifted into infinite space, – all mean egotism vanishes. I become a transparent eyeball; I am nothing; I see all; the currents of the Universal Being circulate through me; I am part or parcel of God." *The Complete Works of Ralph Waldo Emerson,* ed. Edward Waldo Emerson (Boston: Houghton Mifflin, 1903), Vol. 1, p. 10.

26. Thomas Weiskel, *The Romantic Sublime: Studies in the Structure and Psychology of Transcendence* (Baltimore: Johns Hopkins University Press, 1976), Eric Cheyfitz, *The Trans-parent: Sexual Politics in the Language of Emerson* (Baltimore: Johns Hopkins University Press, 1981), and Neil Hertz, *The End of the Line: Essays on Psychoanalysis and the Sublime* (New York: Columbia University Press, 1985).

27. Hertz, *The End of the Line,* p. 76.

28. Patricia Yaeger, "Toward a Female Sublime," in *Gender and Theory: Dialogues on Feminist Criticism,* ed. Linda Kauffman (London: Basil Blackwell, 1989), p. 195.

29. Harold Bloom, *Poetry and Repression: Revisionism from Blake to Stevens* (New Haven: Yale University Press, 1976).

30. Philip Fisher, "Pins, a Table, Works of Art," *Representations* 1 (February 1983): 44, 48.

31. Walter Benjamin, "The Storyteller," in *Illuminations* (New York: Schocken Books, 1969), p. 83.

32. Ibid., p. 87.

33. Ibid.

34. Ibid., p. 90.

35. Ibid., p. 91.
36. Ibid., p. 108.
37. Ibid., p. 109.
38. Sherwood Anderson, "King Coal," in *Sherwood Anderson's Notebook,* p. 214.
39. Ibid., p. 208.
40. Ibid., pp. 209, 211, 213.
41. In particular, see Jacques Derrida, *Of Grammatology* (Baltimore: Johns Hopkins University Press, 1976).

Notes on Contributors

Clare Colquitt, Assistant Professor of English and Comparative Literature at San Diego State University, is completing a book, her first, on Edith Wharton. Her essay on Anderson's "Death in the Woods" appeared in *Modern Fiction Studies* (1986).

John W. Crowley, who has taught at Syracuse University since 1970, is currently Professor and Chair of English. His books include *George Cabot Lodge* (1976), *The Black Heart's Truth: The Early Career of W. D. Howells* (1985), and *The Mask of Fiction: Essays on W. D. Howells* (1989). He has also written numerous essays on American writers, including Anderson.

Marcia Jacobson is Hargis Professor of American Literature at Auburn University. She is the author of *Henry James and the Mass Market* (1983) and articles on autobiography. She is finishing a study of the nineteenth-century American "boy book."

David Stouck, Professor of English at Simon Fraser University, has written articles on Anderson, Hawthorne, Jewett, Fitzgerald, and others. He has also published *Willa Cather's Imagination* (1975), *Major Canadian Authors* (1984, 1988), *The Wardells and Vosburghs: Records of a Loyalist Family* (1986), and *Ethel Wilson: Stories, Essays, and Letters* (1987).

Thomas Yingling, formerly a Fred L. Emerson Fellow at Syracuse University, is now Assistant Professor of English. His book *Hart Crane and the Homosexual Text* has recently been published by the University of Chicago Press.

Selected Bibliography

Several collections of criticism – those edited by Anderson, Ferres, Rideout, and White – reprint reviews of and essays on *Winesburg, Ohio*. Only some of these short pieces are listed separately here. The standard text, used by all contributors to this volume, is Malcolm Cowley's edition, still in print from Penguin Books. Kim Townsend's biography is complemented by several volumes of Anderson's letters, edited by Jones and Rideout, Modlin, Sutton, and White.

Anderson, David D., ed., *Sherwood Anderson: Dimensions of His Literary Art: A Collection of Critical Essays*. Lansing: Michigan State University Press, 1976.

    ed., *Critical Essays on Sherwood Anderson*. Boston: G. K. Hall, 1981.

Atlas, Marilyn Judith, "Sherwood Anderson and the Women of Winesburg," in *Critical Essays on Sherwood Anderson*, ed. David D. Anderson. Boston: G. K. Hall, 1981.

Baker, Carlos, "Sherwood Anderson's Winesburg: A Reprise." *Virginia Quarterly Review* 48 (Autumn 1972): 568–79.

Bredahl, A. Carl, "'The Young Thing Within': Divided Narrative and Sherwood Anderson's *Winesburg, Ohio*." *Midwest Quarterly* 27 (Summer 1986): 422–37.

Bridgman, Richard, *The Colloquial Style in America*. Oxford University Press, 1966.

Bunge, Nancy, "Women in Sherwood Anderson's Fiction," in *Critical Essays on Sherwood Anderson*, ed. David D. Anderson. Boston: G. K. Hall, 1981.

Burbank, Rex, *Sherwood Anderson*. New York: Twayne, 1964.

Campbell, Hilbert H., and Charles E. Modlin, eds., *Sherwood Anderson: Centennial Studies*. Troy, N.Y.: Whitston, 1976.

Ciancio, Ralph, "'The Sweetness of the Twisted Apples': Unity of Vision in *Winesburg, Ohio*." *PMLA* 87 (October 1972): 994–1006.

Cowley, Malcolm, "Introduction" to *Winesburg, Ohio*. New York: Viking Press, 1960.

Dewey, Joseph, "No God in the Sky and No God in Myself: 'Godliness' and Anderson's *Winesburg."* *Modern Fiction Studies* 35 (Summer 1989): 251–9.

Ferres, John H., ed., *Winesburg, Ohio: Text and Criticism.* New York: Viking Press, 1977.

Fludernik, Monika, "'The Divine Accident of Life': Metaphoric Structure and Meaning in *Winesburg, Ohio." Style* 22 (Spring 1988): 116–35.

Frank, Waldo, *"Winesburg, Ohio* After Twenty Years." *Story* 19 (September–October 1941): 29–33.

Fussell, Edwin, *"Winesburg, Ohio:* Art and Isolation." *Modern Fiction Studies* 6 (Summer 1960): 106–14.

Geismar, Maxwell, *The Last of the Provincials: The American Novel, 1915–1925.* Boston: Houghton Mifflin, 1943.

Gregory, Horace, ed., *The Portable Sherwood Anderson.* New York: Viking Press, 1949.

Hoffman, Frederick J., *Freudianism and the Literary Mind,* 2nd ed. Baton Rouge: Louisiana State University Press, 1957.

Howe, Irving, *Sherwood Anderson.* New York: William Sloan, 1951; rev. ed., Stanford University Press, 1966.

Jones, Howard Mumford, and Walter B. Rideout, eds., *Letters of Sherwood Anderson.* Boston: Little, Brown, 1953.

Laughlin, Rosemary M., "'Godliness' and the American Dream in *Winesburg, Ohio." Twentieth Century Literature* 13 (July 1967): 97–103.

Lears, Jackson, "Uneasy Courtship: Modern Art and Modern Advertising." *American Quarterly* 39 (Spring 1987): 133–54.

Love, Glen A., *"Winesburg, Ohio* and the Rhetoric of Silence." *American Literature* 40 (March 1968): 38–57.

Modlin, Charles E., ed., *Sherwood Anderson: Selected Letters.* Knoxville: University of Tennessee Press, 1984.

O'Neill, John, "Anderson Writ Large: 'Godliness' in *Winesburg, Ohio." Twentieth Century Literature* 23 (February 1977): 67–83.

Phillips, William L., "How Sherwood Anderson Wrote *Winesburg, Ohio." American Literature* 23 (March 1951): 7–30.

Pickering, Samuel, *"Winesburg, Ohio:* A Portrait of the Artist as a Young Man." *Southern Quarterly* 16 (October 1977): 27–38.

Rideout, Walter B., "The Simplicity of *Winesburg, Ohio." Shenandoah* 13 (Spring 1962): 20–31.

"Sherwood Anderson," in *Fifteen Modern American Authors: A Survey of Research and Criticism,* ed. Jackson R. Bryer. Durham, N.C.: Duke University Press, 1969.

ed., *Sherwood Anderson: A Collection of Critical Essays.* Englewood Cliffs, N.J.: Prentice-Hall, 1974.

"Talbot Whittingham and Anderson: A Passage to *Winesburg, Ohio,"* in *Sherwood Anderson: Dimensions of His Literary Art: A Collection of Critical Essays,* ed. David D. Anderson. East Lansing: Michigan State University Press, 1976.

Rigsbee, Sally Adair, "The Feminine in *Winesburg, Ohio.*" *Studies in American Fiction* 9 (Autumn 1981): 233–44.

San Juan, Epifanio, Jr., "Vision and Reality: A Reconsideration of Sherwood Anderson's *Winesburg, Ohio.*" *American Literature* 35 (May 1963): 137–55.

Schevill, James, *Sherwood Anderson: His Life and Work.* University of Denver Press, 1951.

Spencer, Benjamin T., "Sherwood Anderson: American Mythopoeist." *American Literature* 41 (March 1969): 1–18.

Stouck, David, "*Winesburg, Ohio* and the Failure of Art." *Twentieth Century Literature* 15 (October 1969): 145–51.

"*Winesburg, Ohio* as a Dance of Death." *American Literature* 48 (January 1977): 525–42.

"Sherwood Anderson and the Postmodern Novel." *Contemporary Literature* 26 (Fall 1985): 302–16.

Sutton, William A., *The Road to Winesburg: A Mosaic of the Imaginative Life of Sherwood Anderson.* Metuchen, N.J.: Scarecrow Press, 1972.

ed., *Letters to Bab: Sherwood Anderson to Marietta D. Finley, 1916–33.* Urbana: University of Illinois Press, 1985.

Taylor, Welford Dunaway, *Sherwood Anderson.* New York: Ungar, 1977.

Thurston, Jarvis A., "Anderson and 'Winesburg': Mysticism and Craft." *Accent* 16 (Spring 1956): 107–28.

Townsend, Kim, *Sherwood Anderson.* Boston: Houghton Mifflin, 1987.

Trilling, Lionel, "Sherwood Anderson." *Kenyon Review* 3 (Summer 1941): 293–302. Revised in *The Liberal Imagination.* New York: Viking Press, 1950.

Walcutt, Charles Child, "Sherwood Anderson: Impressionism and the Buried Life." *Sewanee Review* 60 (Winter 1952): 28–47.

Whipple, T. K., *Spokesmen: Modern Writers and American Life.* New York: Appleton, 1928.

White, Ray Lewis, ed., *The Achievement of Sherwood Anderson: Essays in Criticism.* Chapel Hill: University of North Carolina Press, 1966.

ed., *The Merrill Studies in Winesburg, Ohio.* Columbus, Ohio: Merrill, 1971.

ed., *Sherwood Anderson/Gertrude Stein.* Chapel Hill: University of North Carolina Press, 1972.

ed., *Sherwood Anderson: A Reference Guide.* Boston: G. K. Hall, 1977.

ed., *Sherwood Anderson: Early Writings.* Kent, Ohio: Kent State University Press, 1989.

Williams, Kenny J., *A Storyteller and a City: Sherwood Anderson's Chicago.* Dekalb: Northern Illinois University Press, 1988.